Last Call, A Memoir

Nancy L. Carr

For the Friends of Bill W, and for the untreated alcoholic; that they may read this story and say to themselves, "Hmm, this sounds a bit like my life, maybe I do need help." May they find the courage to get sober - for themselves first - and for others second.

Acknowledgements
I want to say Thank you and acknowledge
those who have stood by me through thick and
thin, and booze and blow, and the good and
bad. I couldn't have been able to put this body
of work forth without your love and support.

To my Mom, for always believing in me and
supporting me and for always being my
biggest cheerleader, she passed in 2012 and
she's my guardian angel today always giving
me the love and light I need from her. I honor
her each and every day by being my authentic
self.

To my Dad and his wife, thanks for being my
hero and my biggest fan in all my endeavors,
especially when I was getting sober. The
support you both gave me through my life has
meant the world to me and having you both by
my side for the good and the bad has been
such a blessing. Dad, you are still my first love
and I'm so grateful you are by my side.

To my sister, for having my back and
supporting me in my sobriety and for never
judging me, even when I probably should have

been judged. Your friendship and love has been a gift to me.

To my Editor, Peggy Lang, for helping me and guiding me through the book writing process. I am forever indebted to you for being the voice of "how to do this" and shepherding me along the way. I couldn't have done this book without you!

To my husband, Liam, for supporting me and loving me – unconditionally – through the process of self-publishing and for holding my hand when I needed it. For reading the book and realizing that was my past and that's not who I am today. I'm grateful we get to do this journey together. I love you.

To my High School friend, Stacey, who has stuck by me since 9th grade and who has been a true friend to me, through the shit and the amazing. For supporting me in my sobriety and being my *healthy and normal* friend who really gets the importance of me being sober and staying sober. You've never wavered on your love and understanding of whom I am and you always have another perspective for me to understand. You get me. Thank you for being my voice of reason.

To Barbara, you've known me since I was five years old and we spent a lot of crazy times together growing up and into adulthood. You were such a good friend to me through all of the BS and lies. I never wanted to disappoint you, but when I called to tell you I was getting sober, your joy was infectious and you've been one of my biggest supporters ever since. You know all the secrets and angst I deal with and you are always there with an open ear. Thanks for being a lifelong friend who I can always count on!

To my San Diego sober posse; Terri, Shanna, Foo-foo, Megan, Bmuff, Sharone, Skeeter, Runway, Kella, and Stacy J: I love you all more than words can even express. You are my soul and my light and your unconditional love and support in my sobriety, my book and my blog has been more than most. You keep me grounded, you give me hope when I feel I didn't have any and you guys all show me the way and help me. I'm grateful that we continue to walk this journey of recovery together. Thank you seems trivial, but thank you!

To Joanne Hammer, you were the voice that was pushing me and supporting me to publish my book, and you've continued to be that voice that is always there with a loving and helping hand. You've given me self-esteem and confidence, when I didn't think I had any and you told me it was ok to publish my honest raw truth. Thanks for continuing to be there for me, you are an inspiration to me.

And to my fellow sober bloggers, my AA family, my sponsors, my sponsee's, and the Fellowships I've been able to be a part of; Thank you from the bottom of my heart! I would not be a sober woman today without all of you and I'm so blessed that I've been able to listen to each of you and learn. You make me want to be a better woman today and I'm so glad I can be open and willing to hear you. You have all given me so much love, hope and support and for that I'm eternally grateful.

Author's Note

This is a Memoir and all facts, feelings and locations are to the best of my memory at that time. When I wrote this Memoir I was in early sobriety and single – and since then I've gotten married and established a career in industry.

Therefore, some of the names and other identifying details of some major and minor characters have been changed to protect individual privacy and anonymity.

Chapter 1

June 1980
Windward Harbor Condominiums
Avalon, NJ

I got drunk for the first time at age
thirteen in Avalon, New Jersey. My memory
of the night is as fresh as the pasta sauce
simmering on the stove. The evening set a
standard of excitement nothing else had
previously touched. My thirteen years
provided no resources to put the experience
into perspective. I had no inkling of
consequences. There was only the thrill of the
moment, blotting out everything else.

Saturday night, and my parents, Robert
and Ellen, were getting ready to go to dinner at
the Avalon Yacht Club where Dad had recently
become a member. My parents, bless their
loving hearts, were wearing their version of
standard Jersey Shore evening attire, a look
perhaps inspired by The Nautical Preppy
Handbook. Dad managed to accentuate his
five feet seven inches in a pair of khakis

bedecked with boating flags. God awful looking pants. A kelly green blazer over a pale yellow oxford shirt completed the image. I remember looking at him quite horrified. My mother's less conspicuous outfit balanced his excess.

What my Dad lacked in fashion sense, he made up for in personality. When he walked into a room, there was a hush. My father was attractive in his own right. He liked to comment that people thought he looked like Robert Wagner - from Hart to Hart – the 70s crime show. I didn't see it – I personally thought he looked more like Frank Sinatra, another one of Dad's favorites. Dad likes to engage people with his quick wit and light sarcasm. His boisterous personality is one that I've inherited, and at age thirteen, I was about to experience a family weakness, a distinct love of the drink.

Alcohol was a beverage that I believed sat on refrigerator shelves as a standard in American households. I don't remember the first time I noticed alcohol, I just knew it was there with dinner, there on the beach, there in the car as a travel beverage, there in the hand of most everyone. It seemed normal. It made sense to me. I would realize years later, to my shock and confusion that not everyone consumed alcohol the way I did or the way most people in my life did.

My mother strode into the living room clasping her clunky charm bracelet. She wore basic beige slacks topped with a conservative pastel collared blouse. Her impeccable makeup and appropriate medium length brown hair gave her style and class. I can still see her spritzing her coif with Aqua Net as her finishing touch. Mom had chiseled cheek bones and large brown eyes. People tell me I'm blessed to inherit her striking features. She looked over at me and my sister.

"Okay honey bunches; make sure you go to bed at a decent hour. Your father and I won't be home too late."

My sister looked at me and grinned. Poor Jenny. I had no intention of sitting home with my twelve-year-old sister and watching TV. I was going to dart out the door as soon as my parents turned onto Ocean Boulevard.

My parents were an attractive couple, but their love for each other was not the comfortable relationship the outside world perceived. I rarely saw them show affection toward one another, but their daily bickering didn't seem unusual. Even then I questioned if

13

my parents could sustain their marriage in the coming years. Most of my classmates' parents were divorced or getting divorced; it seemed to be a trend that was as popular as Rubik's cube.

My sister didn't know that earlier in the day, while I was sunbathing at the neighborhood pool, I was invited to a party given by the older teenagers in the complex. I looked older than my years, and they'd assumed I was fifteen or sixteen. I always felt older than my peers. I felt different. I was not ordinary and felt that great things would happen to me. I don't know why I felt that way. I had an attitude at birth that gave me a possibly unrealistic notion that I could be whoever I wanted to be.

That evening I wanted to be cool, and I wanted to go to a teenage party, and I wanted to drink alcohol. Alcohol, the elusive potion that I saw grownups drink with gaiety and zest, the potion that I saw glamorized on TV and at the cinema, and the potion that the older cool kids were drinking every weekend. I wanted to be cool. I remember wearing tight Calvin Klein jeans with the highest heels I owned at age thirteen and a ruffled white peasant blouse. My dark brown hair was set in a side ponytail, which was trés chic at the time, and it made me look at least seventeen. Black eye liner coated my inner eye lids and heavy black mascara brushed onto my bare lashes accentuated my glowing tan---my first real make-up experience. I'd had no idea what I was doing as I raided my mother's make up drawer. When finished, I stood in the bathroom mirror looking at myself and wondered who I really was at that very moment. I was scared, but felt a surge of excitement as I bolted out the door to venture into the unknown. A teenage drinking party.

As I walked upstairs to the party I was nervous, but before I reached the front door, I could hear Blondie's obscure lead singer, Deborah Harry, blaring from the stereo. Walking into the decadent den of teenagers I could see everyone milling about and laughing. They were drinking from a large circular punch bowl. The party guests all looked to be seventeen or older. I was playing with the big boys now. The choice beverage of the evening was cherry flavored jungle juice - spiked with grain alcohol. I felt like a member of Jim Jones' tribe, belonging and doing whatever the leaders wanted me to do. I anxiously served myself a small cupful and drank it with hesitant anticipation. It was sweet and seemed harmless, no taste of any alcohol. Just right. I walked around, surveyed the room, grabbed a couple of pretzels, and chatted briefly with the party hostess. She was nice enough and had no idea she was serving alcohol to someone still three years away from sweet sixteen. Within two hours, I drank four glasses of punch. I was blotto.

I remember sitting down in a lime green bean bag chair and looking over at the other party guests and laughing. Laughing and laughing, I was laughing so hard I kept flipping my head side to side, and my ponytail started coming out, so I just took it down and flipped my hair back onto my shoulders. I felt like every boy there was staring at me. Male attention was something I always strived for.

The way I felt at that moment was my first "high," a stunning sensation I'll never forget. I was the only person in that room that mattered. It was all about me and fuck everyone else. I would continue seeking this high for the next twenty-four years, a constant throughout my drinking career, always feeling entitled to drink the way I wanted to. Why should I care what others thought about it? Yet in case someone might judge me, I only socialized with people who drank. I only connected with people who wanted to drink as much as possible and as often as possible—as I did. My inner circle of friends and family seemed very accepting of this lifestyle, until I reached a certain point.

Walking the ten paces home from the party that night, I realized I was really drunk. I felt queasy and unkempt. I walked in and ran to the bathroom to toss my cookies. Oh, god, that red cherry punch splashing onto my frilly, white gypsy blouse. This wasn't a vision I wanted my parents or my brother even to witness.

My brother, Bobby, the eldest at sixteen, had just come home from the Bongo Room, the local hot spot where the older kids hung out. Bobby, just getting over his chubby puberty phase, was finding out how much fun it was to be a teenager at the Jersey Shore. He too had a slight buzz after chugging a couple of Budweiser's and wasn't feeling much pain when he arrived home. Bobby was shocked to see me in the state I was in. He couldn't believe his younger sister, the sister who possessed an attitude of coolness, had turned into a trashy teen with makeup smeared on her face in a mere two hours.

My brother resembled my Dad a little with his mild ball nose and quirky smile. His brown hair, curly and full, made him look taller than his medium height. I looked up to him and thought he was cool. His friends were cool guys too. *Cool* was a very big word in the eighties, thanks to Arthur Fonzarelli. Cool Bobby had a pale yellow 1967 Mustang, and he worked as a busboy at the local catering hall to earn his wage. He was your ordinary big brother, either ignoring me or chiding me. He was wearing a white Polo shirt, collar up, red tab 501 Levi jeans and Docksider boating loafers. The trend at this time was the prepster New England look, and everyone around me jumped on the bandwagon. I kept up with the trend for the most part, but just so I could fit in. I had one too many pink and green belts, turtlenecks and sweaters. I was hoping some new fashion trend would hit the market—and soon.

Bobby looked at me, bewildered, and barked at me to get to bed and be quiet. If drinking was cool, barfing was not. Looking trashy was not. I felt like I hadn't really done anything wrong and here he was making me feel as if I had. Going to bed wasn't an option. I proceeded to be defiant and started babbling about needing fresh air. I felt like I had to control my nausea and regain what I'd thought was my new feeling of empowerment. I wanted to see it reflected in Bobby's eyes, let him see how cool his little sister was. I couldn't be seen as a loser, desperate to get his approval. I wanted Bobby to think I was groovy, and I wanted him to like me. I never thought anyone liked me growing up. Sure, they loved me, I knew that, but I didn't think anyone actually liked me. I constantly needed reassurance and acceptance from everyone else in my life also—my dad, my mom, my sister, my best friend, my boyfriend, basically anyone who mattered to me.

I stumbled outside onto the deck with Bobby following "Nance, just go to bed, Mom and Dad will be home soon. You'll be in deep shit." When I heard that I could get in trouble, I got scared and started wailing. My sister Jenny, frightened at the vomit and the crying, wondered what was happening. What the hell was in that punch? Jenny was my baby sister, and she looked up to me. I never caught on to that fact until years later and by then I had already treated her like a leper during our early years.

Moments later Mom and Dad, Ellen and Robert, walked into the dimly lit living room to find the melee going on outside on the deck. "What the fuck's going on here?" Dad inquired of Bobby. I continued crying and my father muttered something about me being stupid and reckless. A little woozy himself, he grabbed a beer and slammed the refrigerator door. The issue of the party-givers and their deadly "Jim Jones" punch could wait until the next day when he himself was subdued. Dad had a temper and used it when he needed to. I felt that my parents viewed my drunken episode as a rite of passage for a young teenage girl. I was never reprimanded, grounded or even given a talking to about drinking, drugs or anything else which should have been forbidden for any thirteen-year-old girl.

I quickly retreated to my bedroom, with my mom following me. While twisting under the covers and going to bed that evening, my mother put me to bed, stroked my hair and told me everything was going to be all right. I believed my mother, as only a child does, but how I wish to God I'd known then what I know now.

Chapter 2

March 20, 2004
The Alley Nightclub
Carlsbad, California

"Lisa, let's vamoose and get the hell outta here. Ernie and I are going back to my Apartment." I slurped down the last of my Absolut and Red Bull and grabbed my purse.

Lisa was one of the good girls who drank conservatively while trying to keep me grounded. We'd been out celebrating my thirty-seventh birthday. Thirty-seven years old and I was still living my life like I was twenty-one. Lisa, tall at six-two, wore dark blue jeans and black flats with a sexy camisole top. When she walks into a room, her Christie Brinkley prettiness, stature and long, flowing blond hair certainly command a glance. I always know we'll be the center of attention when we go out drinking and dancing. I was dolled up for the evening, and shit, if I didn't look like Jaclyn Smith that night. I had always wanted to look like Jaclyn since I was a little girl. Charlie's Angels was my favorite TV show growing up.

My outfit consisted of hip bell bottom blue jeans with black leather high heeled boots and a low cut black shirt, which accentuated my décolletage. I wore my dark brown, almost black hair, bouncy and curly, thanks to my trusty steamed hot rollers and had feathered long bangs with just the right amount of hair serum to give it luster throughout the night. I had made up my eyes with smoky eye shadow, a hint of sparkle at the brow bone and black liquid eye liner, just enough not to look slutty but stay fashionable.

Getting ready for a night out on the town was a task in itself, all done while blaring my stereo volume high enough to disturb the neighbors and prancing around my apartment drinking wine and wondering what the night would have in store for me. It was always exciting, sometimes good, sometimes not, but the night would always provide a story to tell the next day. My *modus operandi* for the evening was always the same, drink as much alcohol as I could consume, hope to score some decent cocaine, and meet a fascinating guy. If not fascinating, at least mildly interesting and hopefully someone I'd want to speak to the next day.

"Okay, Nance, we can leave, but who is the guy standing next to you?"

I smiled, "Just someone I met outside while smoking. His name's Ernie and I dig his sideburns, tattoos and cuffed jeans. I'm going a little out of my normal guy range tonight, and it'll just be fun to hang for a while and throw back some beers at the apartment. Will you be okay with that?" We'd agreed that Lisa would sleep over that night so she didn't have her thirty-minute car ride home.

Lisa smiled her normal whatever-makes-you-happy-Nance smile. "Sure that's fine, I'll just go straight to bed and leave you guys in the den."

Walking out of the night club, we passed by other bar patrons that spilled onto the main street beset with neighboring saloons. Most were Marines, who seemed to have been drinking most of the afternoon, as their loud voices rose above the deafening music emanating from The Alley. The dimly lit parking lot, where my Honda was parked, was at half capacity from when we arrived hours earlier. With Lisa and Ernie in tow, I rummaged through my handbag for my keys and that little voice inside my head started talking to me. *Maybe you shouldn't drive home; you've had a lot to drink today.* Casting aside any rational thought I may have had, I forged ahead and reasoned I was only four blocks away from my Apartment. I unlocked my car door, slid into the driver's seat and started the car. I felt slightly buzzed, not drunk, just buzzed and was pleased with how well I was holding my liquor that night.

Lisa inquired, "Are you okay to drive? If not, I can." As usual, I felt I was a better driver with some booze in my blood stream. "No, I'm good; I don't want you to have to drive my car."

Driving onto the street, I turned left onto the main drag, Carlsbad Boulevard, and told Lisa we needed to make a pit-stop at Texas Liquor for some beer. It was midnight and Lisa and I had been drinking since 5:30 P.M. that evening. Ernie was following closely behind in his Toyota Tacoma pick up. As I screeched into the well lit parking lot, I veered into a space right in front of the store. Ernie parked his truck next to me, taking up two parking spots. He was loud in his arrival. Seconds later we heard sirens and two cop cars drove in behind us and barricaded our cars in.

"Fuck me; you've got to be kidding. Oh man." I look to Lisa.

"Just be cool, you're fine." She reassures me.

I grabbed my wallet out of my purse and said "I'm going to walk in and buy cigarettes." My thought process at the time was not to let the cop think I was nervous about his presence behind me at midnight, on a Saturday, in front of a liquor store. I was going to carry on and do my business. I opened the car door and confidentially walked towards the liquor store. I had this under control. I already had one DUI. I knew a second one wasn't in the cards, not tonight at least. It was my Birthday.

The Skinny Cop walked over to me, "Excuse me Miss, how are you doing tonight?" I gave him a stare that said get the fuck out of my way don't you know who I am. "I'm fine; I'm just going in to buy cigarettes." Skinny Cop moved off to the side of me and didn't say a word. Home free, I thought as I entered the store. The cashier behind the counter looked up when I walked in. He was rotund, Mexican, and wore a name tag.

"Wha's da problemo?" he gestured to the flashing lights outside.

Nonchalantly I replied, "I dunno, I just want to get a pack of cigarettes. Parliament Lights please." *Okay, this is good; they didn't follow me in the store. I can get out of this.*

Behind Miguel, I saw a brown wooden door that led outside to the alley. My first instinct was to run out the back door, but I couldn't do that to Lisa. I didn't want to lose another good friend. Shit, that would have been such a great escape too.

"Gracias, Miguel" I said as I grabbed my smokes and walked outside to see Skinny and Fat Cop questioning Ernie. Ernie, crap, forgot about him. Damn. Before I could even get to my car door, Skinny Cop approached me.

"Ma'am, can I talk to you a minute over here?" Did he just call me Ma'am? I'm not *that* old. "Sure, no problem."

I glanced over at Lisa who was sitting in the passenger seat with a slightly concerned look in her eyes.

"Have you been drinking tonight?" He asked me as he shined his flashlight onto my face, specifically my pupils.

I'd started my night with Coronas, five of them at Garcia's with dinner, switched to merlot—four glasses—at Giblin's Pub, then I progressed to Absolut & Red Bull cocktails—so many I'd lost count—at The Alley. Normal night. "Uh, just a couple beers, that's it." As soon as I said that, I knew I was going to have my ass in the back seat of the cop car. But I couldn't very well lie to a cop that I'd had nothing. I knew my eyes were dilated, and I stank of alcohol.

Skinny Cop looked me over and across my face. "Two beers, huh? I do not smell two beers." Looking to be no older than twenty-four and standing at about five-seven and with sandy brown cropped hair, he looked like a rookie in his standard policeman uniform. But he wasn't a Carlsbad policeman; he was a CHP officer, California Highway Patrol. He looked nothing like Ponch or Jon from CHiPs, another favorite show from my youth.

Shit, the god damn CHP are here. I'm so screwed.

By then I knew I was going to Jail. I was drunk, and they knew it. The only one who didn't surrender himself to the obvious truth was Ernie. Fucking loser, Ernie. He had been yelling at Fat Cop—heavy, balding, at least forty-five. Now, that was old, not thirty-seven.

Slurring his words, he brilliantly sank himself. "Fuck you, I'm not drunk. I've been drinking since 2:00 P.M. this afternoon when I got off work," he shouted to the cop, swayed forward and balanced himself, calling attention to his black biker boots adorned with silver chains and clasped buckles.

God, what the hell was I thinking wanting to take him home? I had hit an all-time low.

"If I was drunk, I wouldn't be here…" He pointed to the Liquor Store sign. "…buying beer and going home with her."

Oh great, drag me into it and tell them that I am with you.

All of a sudden, I got sober. You had to hand it to Ernie though, drunk and stupid and telling the cop the truth. The truth. Humph, people really do tell the truth? I could never keep all my lies straight. Ernie was a real catch. Not surprisingly, I'd picked the only guy in the bar that'd been drinking for the past ten hours.

Skinny Cop initiated the field sobriety test on me, and, feeling confident from having done a couple of these before, I believed I was doing very well and hoped to hear, "Have a nice night Ms. Carr, this has all been a big misunderstanding. Drive Safe."

No, that didn't occur. After I failed to walk a straight line and recite the alphabet backwards, which is hard enough to complete sober, I was asked to breathe into a breathalyzer. Great invention. I blew softly and mildly, only to have Skinny Cop say, "No,

28

you need to really blow. Blow like you're exhaling smoke."

Irritated, I said, "I am blowing hard, very hard. I have a sore throat."

He hands it to me again with a disgusted look on his face, "Please Ms. Carr, blow again." I blew a little harder into the gadget and stepped away.

"Ms. Carr, you are being arrested for driving under the influence."

Oh, is that what DUI stood for? I actually wondered what took them so long. It was five years since my last DUI, and I'd been playing the roulette wheel with my life and other lives around me. Stupid, fucking stupid!

I hadn't fully understood the consequences of being arrested for drunk driving, and it would be months later when I finally would get it. I was very grateful that I hadn't hurt anyone else. My lifestyle certainly invited an accident where I could have been seriously banged up, or worse. Fully understanding that I could be responsible for someone else's life was too mind-boggling. I didn't like myself too much at this juncture in my life.

While being escorted over to the cop car, I could see Ernie in the back of the vehicle, kicking the driver seat with his big black boot.

Are you serious? I have to be in the same car with him?

I was really being punished now. As I was being handcuffed behind my back, reality was hitting me hard, hard like a cold Carlsbad ocean wave surging through the water and breaking onto my face.

I sat down in the back of the car and asked Skinny Cop, "What about my friend Lisa and my car? What's going to happen there?"

He turned around with his pad and pen. "Well, your vehicle will be impounded, and your friend Lisa is going to go back to your apartment. Can you give her a key to get in?"

I saw that Lisa was crying, standing outside my car, talking on her cell phone. I felt horrible. Mad. Why didn't I let her drive?

"Sure, you have my keys. Can you give her my house key? It's the red one on the chain."

I looked over to Lisa, and I was jealous of her, knowing that she would be safe that night, lounging at my Apartment, eating chips and salsa and watching Saturday Night Live, while waiting for me to get out of Jail. Lucky her. I was already longing for my own bed. Skinny Cop got out of the vehicle and handed the key to Lisa. She gestured for me to call her. I smiled guiltily and nodded.

During the drive to the station house in Vista, Ernie was berating the cop as I stared out the window. I was disgusted with myself, not that I got a DUI again, unfortunately, but disgusted because I was with Ernie and my life was pathetic. A sense of doom and dread flooded me, and I had no idea what was in store. My other DUI was during a visit back east over the Christmas holiday, and it was handled by a small town cop, not a San Diego policeman, a CHP no less. I started tearing up and hoped that I wouldn't cry too hard because I couldn't reach my eyes to wipe away my tears. I dug my nails into my skin to pinch myself and make sure that I wasn't in a horrible nightmare.

The nightmare intensified as Ernie inched his way over and whispered in my ear, "I guess this means I can't call you?"

I chuckle. "I don't think so, but what a great first date."

We arrived at the station house where it seemed to be a busy night with other alcoholic felons in attendance. I didn't look like any of them. They all looked like this was a regular occurrence for them, Ernie included. I was pretty sure this wasn't Ernie's first brush with the law.

Skinny Cop wrote up his report and then drew some of my blood. I was grateful that I hadn't scored any coke, and my blood screen would only reveal the presence of alcohol. Grateful also that Skinny Cop treated me with some respect and care. He wasn't rude or demeaning. I felt like a human being for a minute, compared to how they were treating Ernie.

Shortly after giving my tainted blood, I was shuffled over to Intake where a chubby black woman took my vitals. She started asking me questions about my health, as well as my alcohol use and lifestyle. I lied to make it look like this was an isolated incident, and I just had a bad night. She asked me how much I drank on a weekly basis and how much at each sitting. She asked at what age I started drinking and if drinking interfered with my life, i.e. family, job, financial. I lied on every question.

She glanced over at me and raised her eyebrows while jotting more notes onto her assessment sheet. My heart was racing, and I wanted to get the hell out of there. I felt men would show up with white jackets and carry me away. Paranoia set in. I realized I didn't have my Dad there to bail me out this time around. I was all alone, and I had no one to comfort me. It was me. Alone. My family was 3,000 miles across the country and I was sitting in Vista County Jail. I desperately wanted to make a cell phone call to my sister, and I was aching for a cigarette. Neither would occur as they had confiscated my purse and put my personal belongings into a plastic bag. This was not how I envisioned my Saturday night birthday celebration to turn out. Not at all.

If a crystal ball reading had told me I'd be in jail that evening, I would have definitely dressed differently. I always prided myself on my sense of style and being hip. I had all the *right* clothes and adornments, so that I could carry myself in a way I felt most people would find attractive. I was able to leverage my appearance to get what I needed and wanted throughout my life. I was able to get jobs, men, friends, even sales clerks to attend to me in a manner most wouldn't have been offered. Tonight nothing worked. I was just another drunk in jail.

The cell was an eight by ten cinder block wall of coldness. A toilet and sink sat in the corner. I was an inmate with no privacy. A young girl, much younger than thirty-seven, sat on the wooden bench and was resting her head against the cinder wall. Her eyes were closed. She wore cut-off denim shorts, a pale pink tank top and her strewn blond hair was pulled into a ponytail. She didn't look up at me when I entered. She just sat. I tried to sit on the bench next to her, but she didn't seem to want me near her. I moved and sat down in the corner on the concrete floor across from her.

Sitting in the cell I thought again about hitting bottom. I could stop digging now. My life couldn't get any worse. I wanted to vomit, but I couldn't. How could years of my free-wheeling lifestyle as a partier, merely a social drinker, bring me to this place? This was my second DUI and I knew I had to take stock of my life and figure out how I came to where I was. My life looked okay to others on the outside. I had a career, a cozy and comfortable apartment in beautiful downtown Carlsbad, California, and a car, my Honda CRV, which I had purchased drunk after being at a happy hour--that should have been a sign.

I started to cry. And I kept on crying. I
hated crying and I especially hated crying in
public. I cried until the guard, a butch woman
in her thirties came in and said I could make
one phone call. I didn't know who to call or
what to say. The butch guard informed me
that I would be in the cell for ten hours, at
least, that was standard procedure. I didn't
know anyone's phone numbers. They were all
programmed into my cell phone.

I decided to call my sister back East. It
was 2:30 A.M. PST and 5:30 A.M. EST. She
would be awake with my nephews. I had to
call collect, again standard procedure. I called
and started crying again as I waited for her to
accept the call.

She answered in a hurried manner,
"Nance? Is that you?"

The tears flooded me again and I could
barely speak, "Yeah, it's me. I got a DUI and
I'm in jail."

The volume was inaudible and she
sounded faint. She sounded very far away.
Probably because she was. "Are you okay?"

Of course I'm not okay, I'm in Jail. "No,
I'm not okay." I blubbered to her. I just stood
and played with the phone receiver and cried
to her and had nothing to say. What did I have

to say except what she already knew that I was in jail and three thousand miles from home. "I'll call you when I get out. I love you."

Her voice quivered, "I love you too, call me when you get out."

Get out. What *would* I do when I got out? I thought of God and cried out to God to help me. *Please help me, God. I swear I'll be good*. Whenever my life failed me, I would say a foxhole prayer to God to help me, and somehow things always seemed to work out. I needed to know now that I would be taken care of. I relied on my last shred of hope, a shred I would call on again six weeks later.

Ten hours after I was arrested, I was released from the drunk tank. It was one of the happiest moments in my life. Freedom. I grabbed my bag of personal effects, walked outside into the San Diego sun and lit a cigarette. I was worn out. I'd had no sleep and it showed. I called Lisa at my house number, and she came and picked me up in her car which she had left at my house the prior evening. She arrived in lightning speed. I have never been happier to see Lisa in my whole life. I got in and we spoke.

"Nance, it's going to be okay, you're going to be all right. This will be fine. I'll help you in any way I can. I feel horrible."

I couldn't even look at her. The embarrassment of getting a DUI in her presence and the humiliation of having Ernie with me was too much to handle.

"I know you'll help me. Thank you. But this is just fucked. I'm fucked. I could lose my license, my job, I have no money to get my car out of impound. I'm just screwed."

She hugged me and all I could do was sigh. I was all cried out.

Driving away from Jail, we saw a disheveled man walking with his thumb out, looking for a ride. It was Ernie. We flew right by him and started giggling.

"There goes my date," I quipped. At least I still had my sense of humor.

Chapter 3

April 2004
One bedroom Apartment
Carlsbad, California

I am sitting on my couch finishing up a
second bottle of Two Buck Chuck wine, only the
best from Trader Joe's, crying and watching Sarah
Jessica Parker on *Sex and the City*, wondering why
I'm still single. I understand why Sarah is still
single. She spends too much money on shoes, and
no one wants to marry a shoe whore. She had the
perfect man too. She should have kept Aidan and
was a fool to let him get away. Since I was in High
School the perennial question from my parents
and friends was always the same "Are you going
to marry *him*." The feeling that I wasn't married
made me feel less than as a woman.

My life isn't where it's supposed to be.

I'm supposed to be married and living the
high life with my husband who is Vice President
of Marketing for a Fortune 500 company. We live
in a five-bedroom Colonial; have two children and
a dog named Rufus. I'm in the wrong place.

I have been dating since I was fourteen, and
let me tell you, I am tired. Tired of the game.
Tired of getting butterflies when Mr. Wonderful

arrives at my door and I'm trying to figure out what underpants to wear for our second date. I'm easy. And tired of it. I'm tired of trying to figure out what men want. Do they want a relationship, a fling, an affair? I've been in all of those situations and it's exhausting. The not knowing of it all is the most tiring. I've spent more time waiting for *THE ONE* to make up his mind and figure out if he wants me than I have actually spent dating.

My life is spinning out of control and not getting any better. I don't know how to get out. I want to go back to therapy, but they would tell me to quit drinking. I can't lose my best friend. Not yet. Not even after getting arrested two weeks prior for my second DUI. *Second DUI.* Spending ten hours in the drunk tank crying the whole time, while wanting to escape to Mexico as soon as I got out.

I have to swallow the reality that I am a single thirty-something living in America. This excruciating situation is puzzlement for most women over the age of thirty-five. Gasp! *I'm still single.*

Society, family and my friends had a funny way of making me feel like an outcast for being single, so at that point in my life I thought my real problem was not being married! Not once did I think that how I was living my life could lead me to admit that I, effervescent party girl of the eighties, nineties and the new millennium, was indeed a high-bottom drunk, a.k.a., an Alcoholic.

As I now understand it, a high bottom drunk was one who didn't lose anything material. I still had my career, my car, and my apartment. As long as I looked all right on the outside, no one needed to know what was going on inside. *Keep up appearances.* I could have fit in with the Kennedy Clan; Uncle Teddy would have been pleased. But I knew all too well that my mental, emotional and spiritual well-being was close to non-existent. I needed an overhaul. I needed an excavation.

Up until then, I had unconsciously walked through life with a magnet on my head that said, "You may fall in love with me, but you won't marry me because I'm a fucked-up drunk and cocaine addict. So please date me!"

I've had seven serious to semi-serious relationships, all lasting anywhere from six months to four years. Milk has a longer shelf life than some of my relationships. I spent about fifteen years dating a potential Mr. Right. The remaining six years were spent playing the field. I should have spent more time on the field. The field is where I did my best work.

Perhaps because of all the bull shit around me, I was a firm believer that no matter what, the grass is always greener over *there*. Most of my friends were married. I envied them. They envied me. They wanted to go out and meet a sexy hot young man, get drunk and wonder where their clothes were the next morning. Whereas I occasionally dreamed of going home, cooking dinner, picking out fabric swatches for the new couch and making love to my husband once a week. But only occasionally. I didn't want to be tied down, yet I was tired of the freedom.

Some people would turn to family for support. My dad is very moody, though, and when I go to visit him and I'm in the same room with him, I feel like I'm tiptoeing around until I can sense what his mood is. When I call his office, I ask his secretary, "Is Dad in a good mood or bad mood today?" If she says bad mood, I hang up and send him an email. Don't get me wrong; my dad is the most cherished man in my life, and I love him dearly.

I thought of calling Mom, but in some ways her happiness only made me feel worse about myself. After my parents' divorce, Mom dated a man for over ten years, who lived in Florida. We the children, henceforth to be called, WTC, refer to him as her 'convenient' boyfriend—for reasons I need not get into. My mother has a more active social life than Ivana Trump. She has work friends, social friends, bridge club friends, tennis group friends, shore house friends, friends of friends. Over the years, Mom has formed a close group of divorced women, which WTC refer lovingly to as *The Golden Girls*. She belongs to a Jersey Shore group house that sleeps twenty-five people. She is the House Mother. We call it the over-fifty version of <u>*Animal House*</u>. Whoever said life ends at fifty must have been thirty.

If I called my mom to catch up, the conversation was usually fifteen minutes of what was happening in her world and who did what to whom and what she was doing with whom. It was like tuning in to *The OC* for Ellen's life. During the last five minutes of the conversation, you could tell her that you'd recently had a root canal and maybe you both could meet up for a drink soon. It's a wonder she has time to fit her children and grandchildren into her hectic schedule. But she does, always.

When I wanted to see my mother, I had to call her two weeks in advance, and she needed to "check her book." My book, on the other hand, had only birthdays inked in, and the rest was in pencil since everyone was always canceling on me. My mother's was always in ink. Sometimes, Mom would rate her nights and events afterwards with gold stars alongside scribbled comments, "Great time; good food and dancing," or "Fun spot, cute guys." I never let her know that I read her book for fear of her asking to see mine. Mine usually read, "No show, says he had a flat tire," or "Started at Vivo (wine bar) and ended up at Berwyn Tavern (dive bar) and scored drugs." The latter of the two was normally where my night would end up. I would always start my evenings out at a ritzy upscale restaurant or lounge, and by 11:00 P.M., I would inevitably be at the scummiest bar in town. The bartenders knew my name, what I liked to drink and why I was there. Normally it was to score drugs and hang out with the loser guys. I knew most of them and some became intermittent boyfriends. This was my consistent routine the last few years of my drinking career. If anyone was out looking for me; they knew where to find me.

I had reached a point that priests, ministers, counselors, support groups and shrinks see all the time, the point of asking the big questions, desperate for an answer. Why? What was I doing wrong? Was my messed up life really my fault?

Could I stand to learn the truth?

I remember my mother telling me when I was in the seventh grade, "You definitely are your father's daughter." I didn't understand that back then, but today I do. We have a lot in common and our personalities seem to mirror one another.

My parents met when my Dad was fifteen and my Mom was thirteen. They had grown up around the corner from one another in the Bay Ridge section of Brooklyn, NY. They married in 1963, after dating for eight years. According to my mother, who once said to me, "Back then we didn't have a lot of choices. Either you married your childhood sweetheart or you entered the convent." Her best friend is a nun.

I had what seemed to be an idyllic childhood in a charmed world. We started out in Brooklyn, New York, where my dad climbed the corporate ladder quickly, working in the insurance industry. This kept us moving around early in my childhood, and, when I was three, we fled Brooklyn and moved to Palos Verdes, California and then onto Danville, California. We settled back East in Valley Forge, Pennsylvania, and I enrolled in fourth grade at Valley Forge Elementary School. Valley Forge Park was my backyard, literally. I spent many winters sledding down hills and making believe I was a soldier in a mud hut where George Washington and his troops defended our country. We never wanted for anything.

My father is Italian and my mother is half-German and half-Irish. Our family life seemed to work well for us; however, I had nothing else to compare it to. My Father is a true Italian, in every sense of the word. We were the only family I knew that watched _The Godfather_ on Christmas Eve, not _It's a Wonderful Life_ or _Miracle on 34th Street_. It was rather embarrassing bringing home the new beau for Christmas dinner and tree trimming while it was playing simultaneously on every TV. A bloody horse's head resting in the bed of Don Corleone's enemy. Very festive and cheery.

My parents weren't the standard suburban cookie cutter parents, and my perception of how love was expressed between mother and father was slightly flawed. I could say the reason why I'm not married is a heritage thing, but I'm sure that plays only a small part. I could also say it's the divorced parents' syndrome. As a child of divorce, I could be expected to have a more difficult time forming and maintaining loving and lasting relationships. With the staggering rate of marriages ending in divorce, anyone who is a by-product of a divorce may have a better chance of marrying Brad Pitt than staying married. However, I wanted to believe the cinematic love story where the hero at the end of the chick flick movie comes to save…me. I wanted a savior.

How about blaming my pathetic sad life on my choice of mate? I know there are mistakes there that I needed to face in order to learn from them.

Sitting on my couch, huddled into a ball, and slugging the last of my cheap wine, my mind twirled through the rolodex of men in my life. Had I used some of them as pawns as I clawed my way along in the world? That would bring me to the queasy realization that it was maybe mostly me who screwed up. I had to go back to the beginning, rethink where my life went all awry.

Chapter 4

October 1980
Seventh Grade Party in my basement
Wayne, Pennsylvania

My seventh grade party, one for the history year books. My parents went to the Pocono's for the weekend, and Bobby was going to the local high school party. He had a car and didn't want to clean up after a party at our house, so why not go to someone else's house and trash their parents' house? That was the M.O. in those days.

Jenny was going to spend the night at her best friend Hannah's house. Fittingly, my best friend was Maggie, and Hannah was her younger sister. The pair of sisters would, throughout the years, spend summers with us at the Jersey Shore, at summer camp, and we also belonged to the same Brownie and Girl Scout troop. Maggie had been my best friend since we'd moved to Valley Forge a few years earlier. Entering fourth grade, I met her on the school bus my first day of school. I was sitting alone and looking sad, as any child would with no friends after having moved into an unfamiliar neighborhood. Maggie walked onto the bus and smiled in my direction, taking the open seat next to me. My first friend in Valley Forge and she wasn't wearing a colonial frock and hat while churning butter as I'd feared. Maggie was mysterious, naïve, and stunning with olive skin, almond brown eyes, chestnut hair and a radiant smile—much like my own.

I remember Bobby driving Jenny over to Hannah's house – normally that wouldn't be something to have remembered, but since he sat her in the trunk of his car, I remember it quite well. Bobby didn't maliciously put Jenny in his trunk, he meant no harm. He was the selected driver that evening and was tasked with transporting an entire throng of high school boys that resided within a 2 mile radius of our home to the teenage beer guzzling fest. I wasn't concerned for Jenny's welfare since they were only driving her 1 mile from our home --- and since everyone adored Jenny. Jenny was the baby of our family, the charmer. We all looked out for her. She was at her awkward pre-teen stage; innocent, sweet and sassy, her face framed loosely with light brown wavy ringlets and Shirley Temple dimples, implanted into her round cherubic cheeks, gave her an angelic air. Jenny was markedly in her ugly duckling phase, with baby fat still apparent. By the time she entered High School, a couple of years later, she had blossomed into a beautiful and contagious swan. I was jealous of her at that point.

My evening had been planned out an entire week before. I had the luxury of having my own girl's slumber party. My parents thought I would be joining Jenny at Maggie and Hannah's house for a slumber party, but, being the smart 7th grader I was, I decided to have my own slumber party. I had invited a couple of choice boys to make the night interesting. My soiree consisted of five girls, most importantly the leader of our pack and my best friend, Maggie. I emerged as a fashion trendsetter, jock, student council rep and fun party gal with an attitude. I was blessed with a good blend of my parents attractive features; dark wavy and flowing hair, deep set brown eyes and a dashing smile to use whenever needed. Our clique was one that others wanted to join, and we wore the knowledge of our bond with style, charm and innocence.

Certain boys were in attendance, and believe me, they were boys, with hormones surging in waves like tsunamis. They all had nicknames. Fat Matt, Bony Tony, Shorty Sean. I had a crush on a Latino boy in our class who had brooding looks and a slight accent. He intrigued me. The boys brought over a case of Keystone beer, and after sitting around—girls on one side of the room, boys on the other—one of the boys suggested we play *Spin the Bottle*. I'd heard of but never played the scary game where you have to kiss a boy in front of everyone without knowing what the hell you're doing. Panic struck, as *Spin the Bottle* turned into *Seven Minutes in Heaven* with couples disappearing into the storage room of our basement.

The bottle started spinning and stopped at the Latino boy who then spun it again, and somehow, it turned to me. How did the bottle know to pick him and me? Maybe we were meant to be together and would get married. I would have a wedding in Latin America and wear a white flowing organza dress with a long train while holding tropical orchids. This was it. I found my Prince Charming. We walked into the back storage room, and it was oh so romantic with the snow shovel, sleds and assorted Christmas decorations adorning the wall of the storage room.

My seven minutes with Latino Boy lasted about five minutes until I couldn't stand the drool – his, not mine – dripping down my face. I thought of grabbing the snow shovel as a bucket. My first kiss was torture, and I was trying to figure out what all the fuss was about. I knew I had to get my first kiss out of the way and over with so I could be sure I'd be part of the group. Everyone else had paired off, and they were kissing and groping each other. Being inexperienced at age thirteen, I felt like I normally did, the black sheep of the group. Kissing was gross to me, and I felt no pleasure in it. Eeeewww. And that was an understatement.

Soon thereafter I dated Latino boy, and as you normally do in junior high, you accomplish this by having your best friend tell him you say "Hi" in the morning. I was nervous to be around boys and even more nervous to actually have to speak to them. Faced with a phobia of speaking to males, I would eagerly turn to drinking to give me the guts to feel at ease. And it did. I didn't have to put any effort into the lighthearted junior high romance. So, why should I expect that things would be any different in subsequent relationships?

Latino boy and I broke up after three long weeks. He dumped me for another girl in my class—she probably didn't have a problem with drool.

July 1981
Kimberly Miller's House
Belmont, CA

Every other summer from age thirteen to seventeen, I was given the gift of being able to visit my friend Kimberly in California. Kimberly and I met when I was five years old, and we lived in Danville, California. Our fathers worked together at the same Insurance Company, and our families became inseparable for the two years we spent in the Bay area. Kimberly and I continued to remain friends and were pen pals for a few years until we were old enough to board a plane and fly cross-country to see each other. On the off summers, Kimberly would come and visit me.

Kimmy was the quintessential California girl. Blonde hair and blue eyes with a bubbly personality and sweet as honeysuckle. I wanted to be her. For years I tried to emulate her. Her wardrobe, her hair, her music, her lifestyle. I wanted to be the girl that looked like sunshine and exuded coolness and also be a person that everybody loved and admired. I never felt like I was special or that anyone wanted to be like me. I didn't fit in anywhere, so I made up for it by being who I thought you wanted me to be. Pure and standard peer pressure.

My first visit to Kimmy in California was the summer before I entered ninth grade. I was excited to see her since I hadn't visited with her in over six years. Coupled with seeing Kimmy, there was also the thrill of going to San Francisco. My visit there turned out to be one of my "firsts." It was the first time I smoked marijuana—the terrifying substance that all my guy friends were doing and that I was too scared to try. Kimmy had a hard-edged, tough girlfriend, a year older than we were. She had unruly curly auburn hair, and she liked to say *fuck* and *shit* to emphasize her influence. She donned Aerosmith and Led Zeppelin concert T-shirts, and I was scared of her. She wasn't the Welcome Wagon friend I would have hoped her to be.

On Friday night we lounged on Kimmy's water bed-- ultra cool—and drank beer, smoked cigarettes, talked and listened to the newest Aerosmith album. I could tell I was not in Kansas anymore. Kimmy and Tough Girl were talking about girls having sex, friends cutting class and, worst of all, everyone smoking weed and getting wasted. This seemed normal for them. I soon realized that teenagers in California were a year or so ahead of the East Coast crowd. I was later informed by my older brother that trends started out West and moved east. It became clear to me that this was true, as witnessed in Kimmy's and Tough Girl's antics, as well as music on the radio. I'd hear a new song on the radio in California and wouldn't hear it until six months later in Pennsylvania. In my eyes California was the mystical and magical state that everyone talked about. I think that is when my real love affair with California began. Plus, it was where Hollywood was, and I dreamt of becoming a shampoo model, my big aspiration at age fourteen.

Kimmy was a member of her youth church group, which I was really shocked to learn. I just didn't know anyone who voluntarily wanted to join their church youth group. I hated going to my CCD classes at our church and would normally cut CCD to go to the neighboring Denny's for a *Moons over my Hammy* breakfast. On Saturday there was an outing planned with the church group to Great America, the Bay area's amusement park. During the early eighties, roller coasters that spun around and looped-de-looped were innovative. Great America's loopy coaster was only a year old. I loved roller coasters and couldn't wait.

I wanted alone time with Kimmy, but that never happened on this trip as Tough Girl didn't leave our side. Tough Girl wanted to ride the sky ride and I was puzzled as to why, since the sky ride was the most boring ride at an amusement park. When we got on, Kimmy took out her pot pipe and started smoking. I was shocked. In broad daylight? *Have you no manners?* Kimmy passed it over to Tough Girl and then onto me. I was petrified and Kimmy had to show me how to do it. I took the pipe from Kimmy and inhaled like it was a cigarette. (By then I had started smoking cigarettes.) I turned red, started coughing and felt a sharp pain in my throat and continued coughing. After we exited the ride, I was sure the attendant could smell pot in our cab; I was so embarrassed. I didn't enjoy the pot sensations immediately, and that first time wasn't a great experience.

When we got home that evening, Tough Girl asked me if I got high. I knew what she meant, but felt that I never had anything more than a cough and an icky taste in my mouth. I told her *No* and she complained to Kimmy.

"Geez, we're wasting good weed on someone who isn't even getting off on it. This is stupid."

Kimmy looked at me and then said to her friend, "You never get high your first time, and you know that. We'll have her try it again."

We smoked pot again that evening and this time I did experience the euphoria of getting high. It made me smile as I felt myself floating and being transported into Aerosmith fantasy land with Steven Tyler stroking my hair and singing *Train Kept a Rollin*. It was daunting and comforting at the same time, although pot never became my drug of choice as I never felt I was in control. Alcohol let me be loose and groovy, while marijuana made me paranoid and stupid, and it didn't offer the exhilaration and power that my later drugs of choice did. Still, I went home that summer a changed girl, fully dedicated to the partying lifestyle.

Chapter 5

Dealing with two certainties of high school further molded me as a traveler down the party road of life, and I wanted to understand what, if anything could have changed my roadmap. The first certainty was that the juniors and seniors treated sophomores like crap. The older girls didn't like you because you were competition, and the boys weren't friendly to you, not because they didn't like you, but because they still wanted to date their peers. One small advantage was that if you looked or acted stupid, it was understood that you didn't know anything.

The second certainty was who the popular kids were, an elite group of fun, good-looking, sporty and outgoing students. The cliques. My sophomore year began with my clique, the Glum Bunch: me, Maggie, Suzy and some additional choice girls. Suzy was a petite girl with mousy brown hair, nose askew, known to be the partier of her junior high crew. No wonder she fell into our clique. Suzy would later become my life-long cohort.

We emerged as the cool girls who liked to party with the guys and hang out. The other cliques of popular girls were referred to as the Fun Bunch. These were the girls that played sports, were part of the student council and earned good grades—not nearly as fun and relative goody-goodies, but still nice girls. We would emerge briefly as one big group together, but mainly it was the Glum Bunch for me, the ones who weren't the rah-rah types, no cheerleaders among us. We listened to Led Zeppelin, drank beer and smoked cigarettes just like the boys. We could normally be found first thing in the morning, smoking in the breezeway of the courtyard at CHS. Our high school was a ring-shaped building that encompassed a tree-lined courtyard in the center equipped with park benches and a concrete platform where service vehicles were kept. The breezeway was an alley from the courtyard where the druggies and questionable kids hung out, the breezewayers.

Entering my sophomore year, I had no boyfriend, which was slightly uncool. I had heard that summer, while playing in my neighborhood softball league, of a rather handsome fellow that all the girls were swooning over. He was a junior and quite shy. I barely remembered him from junior high, which seemed like eons ago. His name was Brad Turner, and he was voted to the Homecoming Court two years in a row, was Class Treasurer and Captain of the Lacrosse Team. I thought he was appealing, but didn't know what all the fuss was about. He stood six-two, with dark brown hair, light blue eyes, and he was reserved, which is I why I think he was such an enigma to me.

I sat next to his best friend in English Literature, Murray. I never even asked Murray any questions about Brad, since I wasn't fully enamored at that point. Murray was nice to me and would make sure I was being taken care of, and I found out later on that he had a crush on me. When he walked into class, he'd sit next to me and say, "You all right Carr? Is life at the Big C (Conestoga) treating you okay? Anyone gives you any problems, you let me know." He was like a big brother to me, and it was nice to have a guardian angel at my side.

One Friday afternoon in the fall of my sophomore year, Murray told me about a party that was going to be happening that night after the big football game. It was an upper-classmen's party, to which he invited me and the Glum Bunch--a coveted invitation for a sophomore. Older boys, beer and the parents are outta town. We're there!

The party was at J.T. Trucker's house, and he was considered the biggest partier in the junior class. So we knew there would be some heavy-hitters there. Maggie, Suzy and I had brought a couple joints, just in case we needed some reinforcements. J.T.'s house sat on a small cul-de-sac of a barren road which provided ample parking, a benefit; it allowed only a slim chance of getting busted by the cops, an occasional occurrence that could be an inconvenience to any sixteen-year-old sophomore. We arrived after smoking a joint in my Fiat, parked and scampered out; a chimney stack of smoke following us. Walking towards the party, giddy, nervous and stoned, with the garage open we stepped in cautiously and heard voices inside the house. Slowly we opened the door, which entered into the kitchen, to immediately face Brad Turner, and a few other upper-classmen clustered around a half-keg of Budweiser. All conversation stopped. It seemed we'd gone over like a fart in church.

Standing there with each of us high, I thought hours had gone by before Murray looked over at me and broke the awkward silence, "Nance, so glad you guys could make it, can I get you a beer?"

Ahhh…yes, red cups and beer. "Hey, yeah, that'd be great, thanks!" Then the party got started.

I had been eyeing the elusive and popular Brad Turner for a few minutes while drinking my beer and chatting with Murray. Brad seemed clumsy in his manner, but secure in who he was. My friends were in the dining room playing Thumper, a popular beer drinking game (do I even need to explain that?) at the dining table. I didn't want to play Thumper, but standing there and listening to Murray drone on and on about the football game that we had lost that night, I was bored and did what I liked to do best, leave. I smartly excused myself to go light a cigarette, the best excuse to leave any situation, "Umm…I would really love to hear that exciting story of yours, but if you could excuse me for a second I need to go smoke so I don't gag on your story."

"Hey, Murray, where can I smoke here? Outside or in the garage?"

Murray looked at me in an irritated way, and I felt bad for him, but also wanted out of the discussion. "Yup, you can go in the garage or out on the front patio to smoke. No smoking in the house."

Well I didn't want to wander too far away, so the front patio wasn't an option. Stay close to the beer—and Brad. "Okay, cool, I'll go into the garage."

I grabbed my purse and walked into the garage, where I stood and lit my cigarette. Seconds later, Brad Turner entered into the garage. Just me, him, a lawnmower and some old paint cans. I turned and shyly said, "Hi." So profound.

He was holding his beer in his right hand and had his left hand in his Levi jean pocket, "So, I see you're a smoker huh?" This was his way of introducing himself to me? Not going well, buddy.

"Yeah, I know it's bad, but I've been smoking since ninth grade. Old habit I guess. I've been meaning to quit." Could I have sounded any stupider?

"I understand. Hi, I'm Brad."

Really? Only all of Conestoga High School knows who you are. "Nancy Carr, I know who you are. I played softball with

Sharon Drucker. She lives in your neighborhood."

He smiled, "Oh yeah, that's right. Can I get you another beer?"

Swell, he was trying to get me drunk, typical horny kid. "Sure, that'd be grea.t. I'll go with you." I stomped out my cigarette and tossed it gingerly into a trash can beside me and as I followed Brad inside to grab a beer, the oddest thing happened. We actually had a real conversation, not some bullshit high school discussion about parties and curfews. This was a real conversation. We talked about school and the teachers we had, who we liked and who we didn't like. He told me what it was like to be on the Varsity football team, and I, in turn, told him about my softball and tennis experiences. It was nice. He was nice.

Who was I kidding? He was gorgeous. A funny thing happens when men open their mouths, either they're sexy and hot as hell or they're boring and not interesting and you wonder why anyone would want to talk to them. He was the sexy and hot as hell type. After three beers each, Brad and I were still standing in the kitchen, talking and staring at one another. Staring intently, as much as you do when you're young and timid, he finally leaned over and kissed me.

My head started spinning and I thought I was going to pass out. Luckily, I could blame it on the beer if I needed to. Everyone at this point had filtered out into the den to listen to music. We were the only ones in the brightly lit kitchen. The kitchen, small with green Formica countertops and wood-paneled cabinets, had a Norman Rockwell calendar hanging next to the house phone. The beige linoleum flooring reflected just enough light to show off my bloodshot, glassy eyes. Very attractive, fashion magazine cover material, for sure.

The following day I serendipitously ran into Brad at the King of Prussia Mall, where he told me he'd call me that night. He did call me that night and almost every night after that for three years and eight months. He was my first love, and my high school sweetheart. We went to both the Junior and Senior Proms. He would hold my hand in the public, write me love notes and play love songs on the piano. He was incredibly smart and musical and he loved the Beatles. I adored him.

As far as first loves go, they just didn't get any better than Brad. He was special.

Sadly, I sabotaged my relationship with Brad for someone else—someone who would introduce me to a sordid lifestyle, one that I would embrace fully. Brad became my benchmark boyfriend - where no one was able to live up to his perfect image. I hear he now lives in a five-bedroom colonial in the suburbs of Philadelphia where he owns his own tech company, drives a Porsche and is married with three children and a dog.

August 1984
Kimberly Miller's House
<u>Belmont, CA</u>

The summer of 1984 was spent being
with Brad whenever I could. We'd drive
through Valley Forge Park in his family's
station wagon and park to make out and drink
beer. Station wagons were the bedrooms on
wheels back then, the pre-cursors to the SUVs.

Maggie threw a couple of summer
parties at her house where the normal beer-
drinking and pot-smoking had been going on.
Maggie had three sisters and an older brother,
and they made us look like amateurs. The vibe
at Maggie's household was always pumping,
and her home was so enormous that her
mother barely knew who was home and who
was partying. Her mother was very
lackadaisical about her children having parties
as she, too, was a drinker.

I had a trip planned in August to visit
Kimberly in California. I was eager to see her
and be a part of her fast-paced world. By now,
smoking pot and drinking beer were weekend

occurrences with me and my friends, and I was ready to hang with the wild bunch out West.

I arrived at SFO Airport where Kimmy picked me up in her 1978 Toyota Corolla—totally bitchin'. On the drive to her house from the Airport, we talked about our boyfriends, our parents, school, the latest fashion trends and which pop stars we admired. I dug Michael Jackson—prior to his turning into a one-man freak show. We arrived at her house, and soon started smoking pot and sneaking Vodka from her mom's liquor cabinet. Mrs. Miller was a nurse who worked days, and Kimmy was left home alone on a regular basis. Kimmy wasn't friends any longer with the pot Nazi, and I was grateful to know that. Now, she spent a lot of time with her boyfriend, Ronnie who pumped gas at the local fill-up station and had dirty-blond shoulder length hair with brown bland eyes and a crooked smile. I didn't find him attractive at all, but he had that bad boy look; so he was cool. My second night there Ronnie's parents had gone out of town, which gave us the perfect opportunity to party at his house.

Unbeknownst to me, Ronnie and Kimmy had been recreational with cocaine. I

69

was ignorant of cocaine use and wasn't remotely interested in trying it. I was scared of it. John Belushi had just died from a cocaine overdose, and I saw Scarface. Al Pacino made cocaine very unattractive to me. I'd rather stick to pot and beer. As the three of us were sitting around Ronnie's kitchen table making screwdrivers with our Stoli Vodka, Ronnie mentioned to Kimmy about leaving to get the *stuff*. I wasn't aware of what he was referring to at the moment.

Kimmy made a face and said, "Ronnie, are you sure we should get some tonight? I mean, I don't think Nancy would feel comfortable."

Ronnie sneered, "Oh c'mon, let the girl have some fun. She and her friends will be doing this before you know it. We can just have her try it."

Kimmy gulped down her drink, looked at Ronnie, and clasped her hands towards me. "Okay, we'll start her out slow and put it on the tip of her cigarette."

Hello? Did anyone know that I was sitting right there and had vaguely figured out what was going on. I perked up. "Kimmy, I think I can handle this, and no need to talk about me like I'm not in the room."

Kimmy looked at me and smirked, "All righty. Don't say I didn't warn you."

When Ronnie returned with the bindle of coke, I was so intrigued by the notorious white powder that I could barely focus on my screwdriver. He started chopping it with a razor blade on the glass kitchen table and was moving it to and fro with a credit card. Wow. This was real cocaine. The word danger kept flashing before my eyes in neon lights. I felt pressured to be cool and wanted to fit in and neglected the road block screaming *DANGER DANGER DANGER* pulsing in my head.

Ronnie cut out two lines for Kimmy and him, and I felt left out. I was uncertain about even trying this drug. People have heart attacks, overdose and die ingesting this. Why would I want to jeopardize my own existence? Kimmy and Ronnie each snorted up their line and it looked weird to me. I've never put anything up my nose except my finger.

Kimmy looked up at me with a look of triumph and said, "So you can get a taste of this, we'll put some on the tip of your cigarette, ok?"

I looked at her with a look of approval "Of course, let's do it." I didn't want her to think I was scared at all. I wanted to be hip

71

and by now I was curious to know how it would feel. It looked daunting and forbidden, but also fascinating.

Kimmy pulled off the tip of my cigarette and shook out some of the tobacco onto the kitchen counter. She then shook a little of the coke into the tip of my cigarette. "Here you go. Light up, baby."

I lit my cigarette and took a drag. It tasted like sweet smoke and had an odd aroma. It made me feel light-headed. Light headedness wasn't something I was afraid of. Piece of cake.

Ronnie started chopping out two more lines. I looked over and pondered for a minute, should I try this? My hands were sweating but I felt fearless.
"Hey Ronnie, cut one out for me. I may as well try it."

This was the start of my twenty-year love affair with cocaine.

Chapter 6

October 1985
Katharine Gibbs School
Trooper, Pennsylvania

"C'mon Nance, hurry up and snort that line, we've got to make it to afternoon typing class," My new friend Trisha said.

Nothing like doing a line of cocaine before you have to sit at the home row keys and type as fast as you can with no errors. I had befriended Trisha at Katharine Gibbs, the business school I was attending.

I had decided not to attend college in the fall because I wasn't an academic, and college life and going to school had no appeal to me. Neither did I want to squander my parents' money on four years of an education that I wouldn't receive any benefit from. I knew myself too well. I'd end up partying most of the time, and then I'd really be in deep shit. I wanted to start working and making money as soon as I could. At the end of my senior year, I made the decision to go to the Katharine Gibbs School. This was one of the best business schools in the area and typing was my best subject; it just made sense.

My new friend Trisha was dating a local coke dealer. How convenient to have a friend who was connected to the Main Line drug circle and who didn't know any of my high school friends or family. Perfect. I had everyone fooled. Even Brad.

The Main Line is a suburb of Philadelphia beset with blue bloods and the nouveau riche flaunting their status and materialism through luxury automobiles, country club memberships and private preparatory schools throughout the region. One of my friends from high school drove a Mercedes to school, it was her first car. My first car was a FIAT, *Feeble Italian Attempt at Transportation*; and I started it with a penny since the key broke off in the ignition.

Brad and I continued to see each other regularly, though we had different schedules; we made it work at first. I was apathetic about his college party scene though. This was Brad's life with his collegiate friends, whom I didn't know. Trisha and cocaine filled a void for me—one I didn't know I had at the time. As much as I loved Brad, I wasn't fully invested in our future together. I wasn't Brad's top priority anymore, and I felt cast aside for his studies and fraternity brothers. I knew that if I wanted a safe and secure world filled with domestication and marriage, Brad would offer that to me. But I questioned what else was out there. I wanted to put Brad on the back burner and move forward to the hot iron skillet of the unknown.

I took extreme interest and pleasure in seeing how the other side lived, the side that no parent wanted their children to see for fear they could fall into a cauldron of seedy people, drugs and risky behavior. Not that I went looking for the other side; it just found me and I grabbed onto it like a baby latching onto her mother's nipple. I wanted more experiences and excitement in my life, no matter how risky it was. After a few months of doing cocaine, drinking to oblivion, and barely passing my typing tests, it caught up to me. Brad figured it out. My friends at college knew something was up, and my sister had found out—although she too was flirting with the wild side and dating a habitual drug user. It was the 80's--Reaganomics, Crimped Hair, Volkswagen Golfs, Madonna and……Cocaine.

Brad was already attending Villanova and we thought maybe we'd marry in a few years. Of course we did, we were young and naïve.

By spring, Brad and I had deteriorated to barely seeing each other once a week, and when we did, I was bored to tears, literally. I cried to Brad that I wanted more stimulation in our relationship. How many more movies could we rent with a six-pack? My life with Trisha and her crowd was more scintillating. They were older, wiser and poorer. One particular fellow who caught my eye was a local cocaine dealer. He was the Sexy Bad Boy of the group, three years older than I, with ominous deep set eyes and shoulder length light brown hair. His smoldering sinister appeal had the local girls in town panting.

I had decided to break up with Brad and wasn't returning his phone calls, though I felt very guilty about my partying life. I knew I was hurting him and it pained me to keep on doing it, knowing I was losing something that was special and pure. But I wanted to drink and do cocaine more than I wanted to be with Brad. So in typical Nancy fashion, I fled.

Selfish in my wants and desires, I didn't take into consideration his feelings for me. I called him one evening to tell him I needed to speak to him. I could sense by his sigh over the phone that he saw this coming. I met him in my driveway with a box of his belongings, explained to him that I wasn't ready to be with him, and that I needed to take a break for a while. I didn't even have the nerve to break it off clean. Inside my heart, I wanted him to wait for me.

Wait for me to test this lifestyle out and if I don't like it, I'll come back.

Brad hung his head low, hugged me and told me to be good. I broke his heart, only to realize later that I had broken my own heart in the process. When Brad drove out of the driveway that night, I didn't feel any sadness or loss. I felt free.

One week after Brad and I broke up in spring of 1986, Sexy Bad Boy and I hooked up. For the next year, we partied almost every night, and I got to know how his side lived — the blue collar side. I enjoyed it immensely. Or did I just enjoy the coke? Who could tell at that point? I became so addicted to the guy and his drugs that I wouldn't have cared if he looked like Weird Al Yankovich. My life became a constant rush, experiencing blasts of adrenalin with him and his gang of degenerates. I knew that my new crowd wasn't the type I would have invited over for

Sunday dinner. It didn't deter me, though, since I liked the hectic pace and being in the center of the drug network. I felt that I was above these people, and somehow it made me feel better being around them. I was the new *IT* girl of the group. My poor sense of self made me want to surround myself with people that were, outwardly, less than desirable. Somehow it made me feel like the new ice cream flavor at Baskin-Robbins that people wanted to try.

Our weekends started on Wednesdays, where we would go to Casey's, the local watering hole. I was still only nineteen, but I had a fake ID and looked over twenty-one. Sexy Bad Boy and I spent a lot of nights and weekends with Trisha and her coke dealer boyfriend. It was an insidious life, filled with contradictory highs and Spike Lee moments of *not doing the right thing*. I knew being involved in a drug operation was unethical, but I really couldn't make myself care. Being a part of this fast inner circle blinded me to any potential problems.

Sexy Bad Boy and I would deal the coke starting on Wednesday nights. We'd pick it up, take it back to his house, and start cutting it with fillers like the inositol and laxatives used then. I would sit by his side, helping him weigh it on the scale while snorting lines to make sure it was sellable. Sure, that's what I told him. I felt empowered, being involved in our mini-drug ring. It was eye-opening for me to have people know me and what I could offer them when we would enter Casey's. That's where we sold most of the drugs, if not door-to-door service for some regular customers. This is when I started compartmentalizing unscrupulous behavior into the silo of my brain.

I started this obscure process early on in my adulthood, and it spilled over into other parts of my brain later in life. Illicit behavior seemed okay since everyone I knew and hung out with were all dealing or using cocaine; no one looked at any other way, this was the way. Reflecting back now, it makes me sick how cool and acceptable I thought it was. I was still a child at nineteen and ignorance was bliss.

Sexy Bad Boy and I spent our weekends with his friends in Rock Hall, Maryland. This town was small, dingy and simple. It made Avalon look like the French Riviera. Alcohol, drugs and sex consumed our days, and our nights. No conversation. I went to some dark places during our year together, places that only another cocaine addict can understand.

Cocaine is a sneaky drug. You think you can just have one snort, but you can't or rather, I can't. I had an extremely strong love-hate relationship with cocaine. I ran to its solace when I was happy, sad, angry, fearful or just for no god damn reason. I would do whatever I could to get it, well almost anything. I knew I was addicted to it, and I had no control over my using through different periods of my life. Numerous times I tried to stop. I could occasionally control it, yet I always found my old friend knocking on my door. As soon as I sipped one drink of alcohol, I would start craving it. The euphoric and exhilarating sensation I got when I did my first line of cocaine years before with Kimberly didn't go away for me, ever.

The first burst into my nose was satisfying and the drip that trailed it speedily afterwards said to me, "I've arrived." It made my heart race, my palms sweat, and swallowing became problematical. I would occasionally vomit because I consumed too much at once, and it didn't sit well in my stomach. Cocaine, combined with alcohol, gave me a sense of control that I felt I didn't have in any area of my life. However, the feelings of paranoia and terror that consumed me at times were unbearable. Episodes occurred that made me realize the hazards of continued cocaine use. Being young and inexperienced, I didn't want anyone to think I couldn't handle it. The people I knew who couldn't were lightweights, ridiculed by our peers. I couldn't bear to have such a weak image. I wasn't a chump, but my pride proved to be a poor crutch in this case.

Mid-way through my relationship with Sexy Bad Boy, an occurrence that should have been an awakening to the concept that my lifestyle wasn't going to be featured in *Town & Country* magazine took place at a house party of one of the degenerates we knew. There was a small close-knit group that we spent time with, and half of them had homes. Some of these places were dilapidated and grubby, and some were inherited estate homes along the Main Line.

In our Berwyn playground, the environment was always the same, Rolling Stones and Led Zeppelin served as our musical backdrop, and during the winter months playing darts inside was the choice sport, whereas on a lazy summer afternoon tossing horseshoes was the norm, as was drinking, smoking pot, and snorting cocaine. Cocaine was a constant.

We had been at one of the less than stellar homes one evening and the night itself felt dingy, not a lot of gaiety going on, a smaller crowd with few women. I was just one of the guys that evening, and I was longing for some sort of female interaction. It didn't occur to me that evening that our friends could get crass and rude, if they are provoked and especially if they are full of booze and coke. We had started our night at the 6:00 P.M. happy hour at Casey's, and at closing we took the party back to the Berwyn house. By 8:00 A.M. the following morning, Saturday, a lot of the party goers had left, except me, Sexy Bad Boy and the rest of his man crew. During the next ten hours, we continued to party, play darts, listen to music and have long involved discussions about life and how we would solve all the world's problems. Of course, no one even remembered these discussions the next day.

Sitting outside, I saw myself looking into my tall tumbler filled with Absolut and cranberry juice. I was wearing the same clothes from yesterday, and I felt gross. Just plain gross. I looked over to the West beyond the trees in the backyard and saw the sun going down. It was 6:00 P.M. and I had been up for twenty-four hours without sleep, food or rest and the feelings of paranoia started to creep in. This was not something I wanted to share with anyone. I was embarrassed and ashamed, yet also in complete denial that this was a problem.

The final episode occurred before our one-year anniversary. Sexy Bad Boy and I started fighting almost daily, worsening each time. The degenerate crew was sitting around the kitchen table drinking at Sexy Bad Boy's house and it was nearing 2:00 A.M. The stereo was booming Eric Clapton's *Layla* and we had just come home from Casey's, where the partying proceeded through the evening. I had left Trisha and her drug dealer boyfriend at the bar. Trisha's boyfriend was a fucking pain in the ass, but since he was the main drug connection, we had to acquiesce to his every demand. I detested him. He was over 250 pounds, which was odd for a cocaine addict, and had an attitude that mirrored Al Pacino in *Scarface*. He had been acting agitated and

83

paranoid all evening and thought the cops were after him.

Sexy Bad Boy was chopping up the coke onto the glass kitchen table, moving it back and forth into horizontal rows. I hated it when people played with the coke. I felt like I was being teased. Cut it and divide it, no reason to prolong the effort.

Cutting out three fat lines, one of the crew remarked, "This is really good stuff man."

Sexy Bad Boy said, "Yeah I get it from Trisha's boyfriend. You know him, the big dude. He's my main connection, but I'm trying to go around him and work with somebody else. He's a good guy for the most part. He was really squirmy tonight, though I'm sure that's because he was pretty jacked up."

I grabbed the straw from my boyfriend and piped in, "Jacked up, that's what you're calling it? That guy has a vegetable farm growing up his ass he's so freakin' tight." I gulped my beer and pinched my nose and paused. "He is clearly not dealing with a full deck, honey. If you sense it's from his coke use, well then, yes. Call a spade a spade. I don't know what he was like before. But I think he's an asshole."

Visibly annoyed, Sexy Bad Boy looked at me, "Well that asshole is what makes your little world so happy most of the time, so I'd shut your mouth if I were you."

I rolled my eyes and kissed him on the cheek. "Okay, whatever you say. I'll put my nice hat on."

For the next couple of hours, we killed time by sitting around the kitchen talking about football season. The Philadelphia Eagles were vying for playoff space. As a girl, I could hold my own pretty well in sports and carry a conversation with current happenings. Looking at the clock on the stove, I was surprised it was 5:00 A.M. We'd inhaled more lines and liquor than was normal. Hearing birds chirping outside in the backyard was always the sign for me to get my ass to bed.

I yawned and said my good nights and retired to bed. Moments later, someone was banging on the door. My boyfriend rose from the kitchen table. "Yeah who is it?"

Fat Coke Dealer was on the other side of the door. "Open the fucking door, it's me."

Quickly the door flew open. "Hey man, what's going on, what the fuck?"

Fat barged into the house and starting yelling. "Where is it? Where do you have it stashed?"

From the bedroom upstairs I could hear the ruckus and was afraid of what Fat would do. He was a madman when he was coked up.

Sexy Bad Boy sounded stunned. "I have no idea what you're talking about man. You need to calm down. Can I make you a drink?"

Seconds later, Fat dashed up the stairs and threw open our bedroom door. I was sitting on the bed, thankful that I had just put on my bed shirt. Entering glassy-eyed and ready to fight, he ignored me as my boyfriend followed him into the bedroom.

"Man, I don't have any of your score. You're fucking wasted. Let's go downstairs and have a drink."

Fat looked enraged and was sweating like a pig. He ignored my boyfriend and then started going at me.

"Okay bitch, where does lover boy keep his stash? I know you both sit up here and have your lab where you cut it out and weigh it. I know you have your little set-up here."

As he was ransacking the room and looking under the floorboards near the bed, I was thinking I needed to say something to shut the freakazoid up. "Dude, I have no idea what the fuck you're talking about. We do not have our own little set-up going on. You need to chill out."

Fat said, "Oh, please. I know more than you think I do."

As I looked at my boyfriend for some kind of sign, I was scared and without thinking clearly--who could at that time of the morning after a night of too much drinking and snorting?—blurted out, "Well I dunno, check the speakers, why don't ya?" I was scared shitless and wanted to just get him the hell out of the room.

Sexy Bad Boy looked stunned and pissed.

Fat darted around the bed. "Ah-ha, good call. I knew you were good for something."

The speakers popped open and therein lay an ounce of fresh powder cocaine in a plastic sandwich Baggie.

"Yup, just as I suspected, you fucking lying bastard. Stealing my stash and pawning it off as your own. You little prick."

Lunging forward, Fat threw a couple of jab punches at Sexy Bad Boy in the stomach, walked out of the room slowly, and out the front door by the crew who were listening from the kitchen and fearful of what Fat might do to them.

I was shocked that my boyfriend even had the stash, but more freaked out that I blew his cover. I moved over to him on the bed. "Oh my gosh sweetie, I'm sorry. I didn't know that you had anything stashed in there, I swear. I'm sorry, I'm really, really sorry." I started crying.

A few minutes later, Sexy Bad Boy rose from the bed and looked at me with disgust. "Well, you freaking sold me out. Thanks a lot. You little cunt, what the fuck were you thinking?"

I started crying harder. I hated the *c* word. "I'm sorry sweetie, I really am. Are you okay? Do you feel okay?"

Looking more agitated than before, he barked at me, "Yeah, I'm fine, just swell. Cut me out a fucking line will ya?"

On my duty call I shot up and went to our lab, his desk, sat down and cut out two lines. I snorted mine up gingerly and passed the tray over to him on the bed where he snorted his line quick and hard. I looked over at Sexy Bad Boy on the bed. He was in a far-off daze for a minute, and then he slowly turned his gaze towards me. I was a little scared as to what he might say next, so I grabbed my pack of cigarettes and fumbled while looking for matches. Just then, he picked me up by my shoulders and threw me hard against the glass pane door that opened onto the porch.

"Do you fucking think I'm stupid? Do you?" He kept pushing my head against the door as he was speaking. "Do you?" Shove. "Do you?" Shove again. "Huh?"

"Stop!" I started crying and apologizing. "Please, stop" I continued.

He was a man who was coked out, pissed off and clearly ready to break up. He finally just dropped me on the floor and walked out of his room. I was sobbing and shaking and the back of my head hurt. A bump formed on my head coupled with a small wound, the size of a clothes pin. I ended up apologizing profusely again, to no avail. We broke up a week later. Ironically, I learned he was cheating on me with Fat's sister.

Two weeks later I had a mental breakdown.

Chapter 7

April 1987
Paoli Hospital, Detox Ward
Paoli, Pennsylvania

Two years earlier, my parents had finally decided to split up. I was eighteen at the time and had wondered what took them so long. I would realize, in the coming years, how much their marriage and divorce would affect me. I was living with my Dad that April, flip-flopping back and forth between the two. I awoke on a Thursday morning in a panic. A state of madness and fear overpowered my mind. I felt insane. I'd had a horrific nightmare that I'd contracted AIDS from Sexy Bad Boy and was going to die. This was my terror. Sexy Bad Boy had cheated on me with the slut he dumped me for, and we were never careful and had unprotected sex numerous times. I was drunk and high every time we had sex. The thought of being careful never entered my mind. I did whatever he asked me to do.

My father had come into my room to wake me up. Lying in my bed, I was sweaty and cold. I told my Dad I needed help and to take me to the hospital. He wanted to know what the matter was, and I repeated to him that I needed help. He was scared and did what I asked and drove me to the local hospital. Sitting in the passenger seat of the car staring out the window, slowly rocking in my seat, there was no way I could tell him the truth. My family already despised my ex-boyfriend, and to tell them that he had fed me cocaine for the past year would make them go ape shit. Even though I was never forced to shove cocaine up my nose, that's what my family would believe. They would see me as an innocent bystander who got caught up in the fast lane of life, but I liked my addiction to cocaine and didn't want to share that with anyone.

I left my father in the waiting room where they escorted me into a small office. A few minutes later a doctor walked in. He asked me what the problem was. Shaking and crying, I confessed to him that I thought I may have a slight problem with cocaine.

Who'd a thunk ingesting cocaine into my blood stream for the past year would make me have an addiction?

The doctor left the room and brought in the on-call psychiatrist who proceeded to ask me further questions about my state of mind and within the hour, I was admitted into the hospital. I didn't really understand what I was admitted for and or what was going to happen. They admitted me to the detox unit where I spent the next six days with a group of complete lunatics. I still failed to grasp the idea that I too was a lunatic and that I needed to be detoxed. If someone had told me that I needed to enter a treatment facility that would have made sense to me. I didn't understand the difference between a detox center and a treatment center. I thought the only people that went to rehab were heroin addicts, one drug I gratefully never tried, or celebrities.

My roommate in detox had suffered a serious head injury from a car accident, or so she told me. She must have still been detoxing and wasn't all there. Why would someone be in detox for a car accident? It made no sense to me. Did someone toss her from a speeding car one too many times? Or did her drug of choice make her want to jump out? She was twenty-two, had blonde spiked hair, and she talked to herself. It must have been a really gnarly car accident.

At Five East, we were allowed to sit in a central room to watch TV and smoke cigarettes. The thing I liked most was the cigarette lighter. It was implanted into the wall of the TV room like a car lighter. I would walk over to the wall – cigarette in my mouth—and press the button on the lighter, which in turn would blaze up in an orange glow, and then I would position my cigarette into the lighter and relief would settle in ever so slowly. Fucking cool. A vision of Jack Nicholson in *One Flew over the Cuckoo's Nest* flashed before my eyes.

I slept a lot the first few days, as they had given me tranquilizers to settle and calm me. I don't know what they were. I never asked I just took them like any good addict would. On my second day, I attended a meeting of some sort. They spoke about being an alcoholic. I was nineteen and had no understanding of what an alcoholic was. Who were these people and where were they? I never saw people like this. They sounded like a sad bunch. Poor folks. The patients and counselors started talking about addicts having blackouts, which I never heard of.

It was when you drank and didn't remember what had happened. Oh that, right. Sure I had those once in a while. But not that much. I thought the meeting was strange and I couldn't comprehend any of it, since none of it clicked. Clearly I wasn't a drug addict or an alcoholic, I just needed to get some rest and get re-focused on life. I made a couple of phone calls while I was in there and wondered why Sexy Bad Boy didn't visit me. My thinking was still warped, and I thought he hadn't actually moved on yet. How could he? We had been such a great team.

On the eve of my fifth day detoxing, I called my Dad crying and told him to come and get me out of the freak zone. The next day my hero, Dad, showed up and brought Uncle Tony with him. Uncle Tony was a close family friend, and our attorney. He asked me probing questions about the drug dealings I was involved with and I told him our process, how we purchased the drugs, brought them back to the house, and then weighed it out on the scale. I told Uncle Tony, sheepishly, how we would snort a couple lines, to test the product, and then I would start making the folds out of a memo pad of paper I had taken from my office.

I then proceeded to tell Uncle Tony how I would cut the coke with inositol and sift portions of it through the real coke, and how I would re-weigh it and then place half-grams into Baggie seals. I explained that sometimes it measured out to half grams or single grams. After weighing our merchandise, I would put ten to fifteen folds into a small plastic bag to sell later. I further explained how we would patronize the local watering hole and start dealing and how we would both approach our frequent customers. I would sell to the women, he to the men. Additionally, I told Uncle Tony that sometimes I would hold the full stash and Sexy Bad Boy would ask me for it when he needed it. Albeit, I never realized that I was being put into harm's way and that if we ever did get busted, I would be holding the bag, literally. I was rather gullible and thought he trusted me with the bag because he cared so much. If there's a sucker born every minute, I felt like I was in my infancy.

After finally divulging the operation to Uncle Tony, I felt relieved and stupid. It felt really good to unload that from my conscience; but also telling someone else made it real as to just how fucking stupid I was and what I did. Stupid, stupid, stupid. Uncle Tony seemed somewhat aghast when he realized what I had been involved in, but in order to keep my father's temperament calm, he reacted with a knowing nod and shuffled out of the room.

I got out of detox that Saturday afternoon. That night I went to a party and scored some coke. I was back in the saddle once again. I hadn't learned a thing. Let it ride, baby.

Chapter 8

April 1988
Mother's House
Chesterbrook, Pennsylvania

I used to say to myself, "I'm only going out for one drink, maybe two, that's it." Hours later I'd be awake, using, still drinking, and keeping company with seedy people that I would never want to be seen with during the daylight hours. This extended partying would always leave me with that same feeling of despair, dread and bewilderment as to how I got to that place. I was a chameleon and could morph into anyone I needed to be in order to get what I wanted. It was always all about me, and fuck everyone else.

Looking back on my time with Sexy Bad Boy, I realize it was my genesis into an existence shrouded in alcohol and drugs. My life had many happy and pleasurable moments, but more often than not I was always searching for something to fill the black hole, the void in my life. It was men, it was work, it was money, it was shopping, it was food – but predominantly it was alcohol and coke that fixed me and gave me a feeling of completeness. This existence became as routine to me as a morning Starbucks fix.

I ran into Sexy Bad Boy and his bride at the mall about fifteen years ago. They live above a topless bar in Spring City, Pennsylvania and have two children. He looked bloated, wearing an Eagles jersey covered by his stylish Members Only Jacket. A shame I let him get away. She looked even scarier, an Elvira with a menacing glare, not an appealing person to be around. I immediately thought of Mimi from the Drew Carey show, but after a better view of her pear-shaped body and her teased tri-colored hair, she just screamed *trailer park's finest* to me. It took me a while to figure out why I would get dumped for her. I had a hard time absorbing the truth that I was dumped for someone that I felt was less than me. I didn't want to feel abandoned for someone else, regardless if they were right for me or not. I had lost. I was defeated. But, in reality though, that lifestyle wasn't to be mine.

After the dumping from Sexy Bad Boy and my stint in detox, I moved back in with my mother. I wanted my caretaker back. However, my mother was going through her own ordeal, the divorce from my father. She was depressed and sad, and I couldn't do anything to comfort her. I didn't know how to. I didn't have a caring bedside manner and was very selfish in my own wants and needs. When it came to matters of the heart, I didn't know how to help myself, let alone anyone else. I retreated into my social life and went on my merry way.

Now twenty-one, I had been fooling my employer for two years that I was a diligent and hardworking individual. Most of the time I was, but towards the end of my job stint, my work ethic was suffering. I had been working as a secretary for a prominent real estate developer in King of Prussia. My boss was understanding when I had to go into detox, and welcomed me back with open arms. But, I wasn't able to forgive myself and was embarrassed that my colleagues had known what I had done. I became a mediocre employee and started losing my motivation to continue working, although I was making a decent salary, which in part allowed me to have a surplus of money as my only expenses were for my car and a minimal amount I gave to my mom for rent. This surplus left me with plenty of cash for partying materials.

In between my Monday through Friday nine-to-five job, I had a penchant for sowing my oats. I was out almost every night of the week and I was a flirt. I barely remember any of the men during this time, some vague faces, but mainly they were just your typical wastoids. I was swimming in a sea of sludge and drowning rather quickly, but I didn't care. I had such self-loathing for what I had become, but my destructive life was the only one I knew. I kept on telling myself that if I could get a better job, a better boyfriend, a better car, a better wardrobe, a better hairstyle, I would be better. I would keep on searching until something else stuck. I scattered myself amongst different classes of people to keep up my facade.

I had three different groups of people that I spent time with; this way I was never overexposed to the same clique. There was the party crew I still knew from the Sexy Bad Boy days, the leftovers from high school and the bar fly's I had picked-up locally.

I quickly escaped into blurry nights with people I didn't know nor should I have been with, men particularly. I was looking for love in a garden full of overgrown weeds rather than in a meticulous pruned rose garden. I clearly was looking through glasses that weren't rose colored, but clouded with disillusionment. If you put some of the men that I slept with during this time in a line up, I would be lucky to remember even one of them. I was drinking at dive bars a lot and doing as much coke as I could find. I was slacking off at work and arriving late frequently. I was also gaining weight. My self-respect was dwindling, and I was still filling my black hole with food, drugs and alcohol. Even though I was doing a decent amount of cocaine, I still gained weight. When I would come down from a long night of partying, I would be so ravenous the next day that I would crave salty fatty foods. I would take a four day hiatus from coke and would eat to fill my empty space.

My close high school friend Suzy was attending Penn State College in Happy Valley, Pennsylvania. A four hour drive from home, I would make weekend road trips and visit her frequently to party. She and the rest of the Glum Bunch were concerned about my lifestyle, as well as my physical appearance. Suzy was dating a mutual friend of ours at home while she was away at college. His name was Sean, with icy blue eyes and a sexy smile, someone you looked at twice. He also annoyed the shit out of me as he was dim-witted and lacked basic conversation skills. I liked to think I was fairly intelligent and could maintain a façade of intellect.

From time to time, Sean and I would get together to drink and snort coke, and he was always very nice and flirtatious with me, which was a boost to my self-esteem. One evening we went out for a few drinks and scored some coke. We drove into a neighborhood park to cut out some lines, where we sat in my car and listened to Peter Frampton, *Baby I Love Your Way*. I can't listen to that song to this day. It brings me back to that evening in the car, one I've tried to erase from my brain. We were drinking beer from our six-pack and snorting lines furiously. Drinking and cocaine made me amorous, and I was able to infuse loving feelings for the person I was sitting next to. Pretty soon Sean and I started kissing. Kissing led to more kissing and more kissing led to me taking off my pants, and next thing I knew we were having mad crazy sex in my car.

Shit! My god! This was Suzy's boyfriend. Worse yet was that I didn't have that feeling of guilt or regret until the next morning when I woke up. When I came to, I started making phone calls to run damage control in the hopes that Sean didn't share our escapade with anyone. Too late. Hours later Suzy called me crying and yelling.

I tried to deny it at first, but she told me that a reliable source had called her. I did say Sean was dim-witted right? I knew I was screwed. I was mortified; this was unspeakable. Those feelings of remorse and shame, which by now were a normal occurrence, arose again, and I wanted to die. I wanted to run away and leave everyone and everything behind. What kind of a friend does this to one of her closest friends? The worst kind. I knew it was wrong to do this, and the consequence I would pay, for possibly losing one of my closest friends, vanished completely from my mind. My rationalization was that Suzy attended college four hours away and only saw Sean once a month at best, so they weren't in love or anything. *What's the big deal?*

The following month the Glum Bunch came home for summer break. We had planned a night out at one of our favorite nightclubs. Suzy barely spoke to me, and rightfully so. Everyone else also seemed to keep their distance from me. I just drank and snorted coke all evening and pushed my ill-considered actions onto the back shelf of my conscious mind, as I did with all shameful and regrettable acts. My back shelf was beginning to pile up.

The next morning at 10:00 A.M., my mother woke me and told me there were some people waiting for me in the kitchen. I thought I had skipped out on my bar tab the prior evening, and they were there to collect. She told me there were donuts and coffee. My overweight physique needed fuel, and I sprang out of bed.

Yawning, I walked into the kitchen, and sitting around the kitchen table were Bobby, Jenny, Maggie, Suzy and a few others from the Glum Bunch. I looked like shit and was embarrassed that everyone saw me wedged into my too small pajama bottoms and oversized T-shirt, covering up my plump body. I had ballooned up to 198 pounds.

"What's going on?" I stammered as I grabbed a donut and coffee.

I was very confused and knew this wasn't a good thing. I took a seat at the kitchen table where my family and friends performed an intervention on me. They each went around the table, saying what I had done to hurt them. I couldn't fucking believe this. I felt they had all hurt me and deserted me when they left for college to move on with their lives. I was embarrassed, humiliated and ashamed. I started to cry for what I had become and also because I realized that they truly did care about me, they just didn't know what to do with me. I felt they were more concerned about my weight, though, than my personal well-being. I was raised that as long as you looked good on the outside, no one knew what was going on inside. The sad part was I didn't look good on the outside, and I never shared what was inside. It would take me eighteen years to figure out that I might need to work on my insides first.

Suzy was hurt that I had slept with Sean and my family thought I was drinking too much. However, no one ever offered me any help on how to fix me. No one said you need to tend to your drinking and drugging. There was no solution to the intervention. I felt the attitude was *shape up and get your act together*. That was the message. I can't fault anyone for that. I fault myself for not recognizing my real problem, but I was too scared to say anything. Although, I didn't want to stop drinking or doing coke, and no one could have stopped me.

My family had their own issues in life to deal with, and they too were scared. I think we were all very ignorant as to how to deal with alcohol and drug abuse. It was socially accepted and prevalent in all of our lives, at least the drinking part. No one had informed my family that I was still drugging on a regular basis. My family and friends drank, and this was my party phase that everyone went through in their early twenties. I was just made the example. I felt like a scapegoat since my friends were telling me I needed help, and they didn't seem to recognize that we had all just gotten shit-faced together the night before and had chipped in to buy an 8-ball of coke for the weekend.

The same thing occurred when I left detox after my cocaine breakdown. No solution was offered to me, not that I would have taken one. I ended up going to psychotherapy for two months after the intervention. I lied the entire time to my therapist about my drinking and using, and then I just stopped going. I told her what she needed to hear to report back to my parents, and that it was just an experimental phase I had with cocaine. It wouldn't happen again.

Just dry her out and get her back to life.

My mother took me to Jenny Craig and I consciously started to lose weight. I let up a little on the partying for a bit, but was soon fired from my job for not being able to make it to work on time. I started working temporary administrative positions, but I wasn't happy with any of them. I was spent, bored and just wanted out. Again, I wanted to escape, but this time I wanted out of Pennsylvania.

I felt like I needed to really find myself. A fleeting thought entered my mind to join the Peace Corps to save souls in an impoverished third-world country, but redemption for me wouldn't be found in digging trenches for clean drinking water. I realized that this alcohol and cocaine problem might be an issue, and I wanted to clear my head. My father, who was rather disgusted with me at this point, decided a move away would do me some good. He felt that if I had a fresh start somewhere else, I would be able to get back a semblance of a life and become a productive member of society. My dad wasn't one to address issues with communication. He was an action man and always came to my rescue as my hero. Enabling was part of my family's dysfunction, and all my family wanted to do was take care of each other. We just didn't know how to without putting our hands into your bowl of mush.

The relationship between my father and me was slowly evolving into a grown-up father and daughter relationship, where a mutual respect and admiration for one another was emerging. Granted my dad wasn't happy with where my life had taken me, but he started treating me as a young adult and not as a child. I could sense he felt guilty about the divorce and was trying to make up for lost time when he was absent throughout most of my childhood. After being scared of my father for many years, and though it wasn't until I entered my late teens that I truly began to value what my father represented to me and our family, I finally understood better the sacrifices he had to make in order to be the provider and boss of the family. The reason he worked six days a week and most evenings, was because he had to. He had to prove to himself and his family that he could rise above the odds of living in a struggling environment among working class immigrants in his New York neighborhood. A young boy who started working at age nine with a paper route and no promise of a college education on the horizon. Determination, perseverance and motivation were his main drivers, and Dad wanted to be the bus driver. He had the hunger to be somebody and took it to an obsessive level of immoderate perfection.

Burgeoning through his corporate career, Dad ended up driving himself so hard that he hit a wall and stopped. At about the same time he and my mother split, Dad quit his executive management role at the financial institution he managed and started his own company. Breaking free from the prison walls of corporate America, Dad was able to make his own rules and be his own boss.

My dad mellowed after he and my Mom divorced and seemed calmer and more grounded in his ways. His drinking settled down, and he didn't us it as much as an escape vehicle, but more as a social lubricant. He and I started spending more time together, though we weren't going to attend the next Father-Daughter dinner dance at the Italian-American club. Yet I felt a sense of gratitude for his being my father and becoming a mentor and friend to me.

I could be around Dad and love him, in spite of our earlier relationship. I learned that he and I were very much alike, in the way we handled people and situations, the way we enjoyed living life with gusto. I learned a great deal about business and work ethic from my father. The day I turned sixteen, he had me canvassing the mall to apply for my first part-time job. Dad taught me the value of a hard-earned dollar, and with that I gained a certain sense of how to be an employee and accountable. However, I wasn't exactly a shining example yet.

Our newfound closeness may have helped me change my ways, which would never be conservative in comparison to other people I knew. My father and I socialized together and would dine out at fancy restaurants and drink with one another, and we could charm the champagne right out of your flute. I learned how to be a charmer from my father. I also learned to embrace each minute of life as if the clock was ticking towards midnight and you had only minutes left until you turned back into a pumpkin.

Chapter 9

Aspen, Colorado, notorious playground for the rich and famous, my first out-of-state geographic and the first time I was away from home and living on my own. I was truly alone and living in a world full of alcohol and drugs. I thought if I could move away from home, I would be leaving the real problem behind. Not once did I think I was the problem. The problem was everyone else. Moving to a place of scenic beauty gave me the illusion that my life could be better. I didn't want to change the way I was living, I just wanted to change where I was living it. If I could transfer my lifestyle and insert it into a different location on my spotted roadmap, maybe things would get better. Also, let's not forget the fact that in not looking inside myself for the causes, I was still blaming my *not married* issue on my choice of mate, not my lifestyle.

Party, party, party.

I had spent recent summers and spring vacations in Aspen with my childhood friend,

Maggie. Maggie and I had sustained our close friendship after High School where I would visit her at college and talk to her on a weekly basis. Being the first friend I made in grade school, our unconditional friendship for one another was like an ongoing emotional embrace. Maggie's father owned the majority of Aspen with his holdings consisting of hotels and commercial real estate. My prior visits had included great skiing, fancy restaurants, and of course, the main attraction, partying which was non-stop and standard in this spirited and exclusive village. Aspen is a small community made up of local career residents; real estate agents, interior decorators, bankers and millionaire entrepreneurs. It's also a working class town where bartenders, ski instructors, waitresses and aerobics instructors made their living. Besides being one of the most beautiful places in the country, Aspen offered something for everyone. During the summer months it was more low-key and not as touristy. The lush and gleaming Rocky Mountains with the Roaring Fork River surrounding town offered horse trail rides and whitewater rafting, which I'd enjoyed on prior visits. I preferred summer in Aspen to winter. It wasn't as glitzy as the winter wonderland playground which catered to the upper echelons of society. At 11,000 feet above sea level, Aspen gave you a head rush like no other. You could feel the lack of oxygen when you had a drink, when you smoked a cigarette, went hiking, or, in my case, came stumbling home after an evening out.

I moved to Aspen and barely knew anyone, except Julia. Julia was Maggie's older sister, and she was the Paris Hilton of her time. Beautiful, funny and engaging; you wanted to be in her world. I was. For a bit. I held three jobs where during the daytime I was a loan assistant at the local Aspen bank, and three nights a week I waitressed at a mediocre Italian restaurant, and two nights I made pizzas for a take-and-bake pizza joint. Not a lot of time for fun. Hardly, the fun was when you worked.

You drank when you worked. On Fridays at the bank you started drinking at lunch and zinged off a couple lines of coke. Normal corporate lifestyle. Everyone I worked with was young and eager, and there wasn't a lot of supervision at any of my jobs. The supervisors were, in fact, the catalysts.

Pitkin County Bank, controller of money for the wealthy and famous citizens of Aspen, was where I would spend my days. I was a

Loan Assistant and my boss was a Loan Officer. She was five years older than I and would arrive at work haggard and tired most mornings, looking like she rolled out of bed, threw on a pair of leggings and grabbed the first baggy sweater she could find to drape over her plump frame. I was taken aback as to how certain business practices were conducted. There was no sense of business presence or professionalism displayed. I deduced that people in Aspen, to be specific, worked differently than others on the East Coast.

Typically on Friday afternoons an open bar was set up in the lunch room for certain staff members. After the alcohol would take effect, thirty minutes or so, some co-workers would retreat to the bathroom to snort some coke. My boss led this effort and within a couple of weeks, I was given a VIP invitation to join her and a couple other colleagues. These early Friday happy hours would continue on at the local bar across the street after the work day had ended. No one was ever questioned as to how or why this kind of behavior was tolerated; it was just accepted as part of our working day at the bank. It suited me fine as I was keen to partake. The same work ethic flowed into my other jobs I held in

Aspen; waitress, hostess, pizza twirler -- all held the same moral standards while you worked.

During this period, I was modestly managing my weight issue and had slimmed down to 170 pounds, although I wasn't as fit as I wanted to be. The people I met were vastly different from my East Coast crew. My new friends were from different sectors of the world, except the one person I met from Pennsylvania, and I really felt we connected. We actually didn't at all, but I wanted to feel like I was home.

They hailed from New England, New Zealand, New Jersey, New York, Massachusetts, California, Boston, Atlanta, France, Australia and the U.K. I felt more in touch with the people from the U.S., and everyone had a sad story, or so it seemed. I befriended a British girl who'd moved to Aspen two years prior. She was a blonde beauty and petite in stature. Five years older than I, she seemed to have her life together. She drank in a sophisticated manner and kept the boys at bay with her mysterious attitude. In reality, Brit Girl had fled her country to find her father who had left her when she was four. Her mother had three younger brothers to tend to and wasn't able to give Brit Girl the attention or love she needed. She met a man, fifteen years her senior, and became his mistress. He lured her to Aspen, where he had a looming drug addiction which required her to engage in. She too couldn't get out of the tight grip of cocaine. Brit Girl and I spent many an evening together after we finished our waitress shift. She soon fled Aspen and moved to New York City to become an actress. We swore we'd keep in touch. I never heard from her again.

I lived in the center of town at the Aspen Club Lodge, a hotel that Maggie's Father owned. Julia lived across the hall from me and we walked everywhere and partied our asses off. I met a lot of interesting people through Julia. Every day was a new adventure in which I continued to medicate myself with plenty of alcohol, cocaine, marijuana, LSD, Ecstasy, Quaaludes and magical mushrooms.

One evening, Julia invited me out with her friends to the Paragon, the cool hip nightclub in town. There was a CD promotion party for the new Rolling Stones album, *Steel Wheels*. It was being given by the local Aspen radio station, and Julia knew the right people to get us a VIP table. Julia's friends, mostly trust fund children and free spirits, all held menial jobs and liked to experiment with various life styles. Sitting at the Paragon, we were seated at a round table and I was drinking Julia's newest concoction: a double Absolut on the rocks with a lemon squeeze. It wasn't as strong as I thought it would be. This beverage became one of my choice cocktails for the next fifteen years.

Julia's boyfriend strode in with two good looking guys in tow, three boys and three girls. Convenient. Julia took out her flask and started sipping from it. *How gauche, can't she just order a drink from the bar?*

I looked at her with an annoyed look. "What are you doing? Can't you just order Vodka here like a normal person?"

Julia's eyes were lit up like a Christmas tree. "Nance, man, it's 'shroom tea, it's not booze." She laughed at me like I was brainless.

"Oh right, of course it is."

Soon thereafter Julia was passing the flask around the table, and we all started taking sips. You could do anything in this town, and no one cared. There were no chaperones. I don't know if I ever even saw a policeman in Aspen.

The music was pumping The Stones' newest album and lights were flashing throughout the club. I was hoping we could leave soon as I never liked to stay at one place too long, and I wasn't a fan of nightclubs. Never being able to get my drinks fast enough, I preferred the solace of a bar, usually a dive bar where you can get your drinks quick and pain free. No standing in line and no waiting for a waitress.

Surveying the club for any exciting people to flirt with, I decided to just focus on the boys at our table. One of interest to me was Limo Boy, who worked as the limousine driver for the Aspen Club Lodge. I knew he looked familiar as he picked me up from the Airport a few days prior. Limo Boy was medium build with dark wavy brown hair and soft brown eyes. He was a ski bum and, to a tired and semi-sober woman arriving off a four hour plane ride, he wasn't much to look at. He got cuter as the evening wore on, and shortly after I gave him the once over, he sauntered over to me and made the obligatory small talk.

"So how's it going?" he asked as he leaned across the table and toyed with his beer bottle. I was less than impressed with his opening line, but after three double Absolut's

118

and some of Julia's magical tea, I was feeling no pain. Limo Boy and I were flirting a bit and chatting with everyone else at the table. I was getting bleary-eyed and wanted a change of scenery, and Limo Boy seemed to be carrying his own rather well. I figured he probably had some coke. More reason to leave with him. I suggested that we go to Cooper Street bar, which was around the corner, and he agreed.

Cooper Street was where the locals hung out and also where you could score some coke. The customers were playing pool and drinking beer. Crushed peanut shells covered the floor, and drunkards danced and swayed around the juke box. We sat down at the bar, ordered two beers and started talking. Limo Boy was cute at this point in the evening, one of those guys who grew on you. I was interested and put on the charm for him.

"I think it's great that you came out here with a vision and you are following it. That takes some real discipline. You're going to do well." I lit up a cigarette and blew smoke rings towards him. "When are you planning on opening up your snow board shop?" Men love talking about themselves.

Limo Boy was eating the peanuts from the bar. He sat up and split one with his forefingers. "Thanks. I think it'll work out well. I have my father putting up the capital, and I just secured a lease for the shop around the corner near Little Nell. Hopefully we can open up by October, right before the season. It'll be sweet."

He ordered us two more beers and we moved over to a table in the back away from the riff-raff. A guy with a plan. I was sucking in my stomach at this point, so I didn't feel so overweight, but knew that I wasn't going to win a bikini contest anytime soon.

"So, what's your story?" he asked. "I just picked you up at the Airport, what thirty-six hours ago?"

I could tell he was trying to size me up. His questions clustered around getting me to reveal whether or not I had any family funds to speak of. I was starting to get antsy and really wanted to do a line. I glanced down at the table and picked up my cigarettes and lit up again.

"Oh, I've been vacationing here for years with Maggie's family. Maggie is my best friend from home, and well, let's just say I needed a change. I've got a couple jobs right now. So, I think I'll fare okay. Julia's dad has us living at the Aspen Club Lodge, so that's pretty cool." I scoped the perimeter of the bar, looking for anyone I may know, hesitated a bit, gulped down most of my beer, and finally peered at him as if telling a secret. "So do you know where we can get any blow around here?"

Limo Boy fidgeted a bit in his seat and looked back at me. "Yeah, I've got some right here. You can go have a taste. We can get some more soon too. My connection, the local taxi driver in town, he'll be here soon, and we can hit him up." Limo Boy put the seal of coke on the table under his hand and slid it away.

I snatched it from his grip. Getting up from the table to walk to the bathroom I turned towards Limo Boy and said, "That's what I love about this town. You can call a fucking cab driver, and they deliver drugs to you. How brilliant is that?"

Limo Boy looked at me in a flirty way, "Do you mind if I join you in the ladies room?"

I was a little surprised but realized anything goes in this town.

"Really? Okay, sure. It's your stuff."

We walked inside and could hear two female patrons snorting a line and talking about how hot the bartender is. We walked into the other stall. Limo boy cut out two fat lines, and we snorted 'em.

"Pretty good huh?" Limo Boy pinched his nose.

I took a sigh and flitted my nose a couple times. "Oh my, very good. Aspen has the best stuff anywhere. I know why now it's called the cocaine capital of the country."

Limo Boy laughed and cut out two more lines, and we hit 'em again. I leaned against the bathroom stall and looked up at the ceiling while Limo Boy leaned over and started kissing me. Before I knew it, we were full-on mashing. I saw Limo Boy a couple more times after that. We did what I knew how to do best. Party and have sex.

Aspen was a very strange place for me. A lot of drugs and a lot of odd and disposable people I would never see again who would probably die a slow and tortured death from AIDS or alcohol and substance abuse, while others would flourish in the fast lane of life until they would hit a wall. Some would get smart and leave and some would become suburbanites who would have their crazy Aspen experience to gloat about to others. I had lived a rather sheltered life until Aspen. I was scared of what else was out there that I hadn't experienced. Life became too difficult for me to deal with. I wanted to just run home and go back to the life I was living. At least I knew the scene back home, and I had my friends and family to make me feel normal, for the most part. I left after nine zany months, and it was one of the better decisions I ever made. I was twenty-two years old and thought I was going to die – yet again – from partying too much or from AIDS. Both scared the shit out of me.

Chapter 10

December 1988
Maggie's house
Villanova, Pennsylvania

After I came back from Aspen, I wanted to rest and spend time with my family and friends. Specifically, Maggie. Maggie had been diagnosed with angio sarcoma while I was in Aspen. Cancer of the connective tissue. I was numb and didn't know how to handle news like this. We were almost twenty-three years old and starting our lives. How did someone as beautiful, smart and lively get cancer? It didn't make sense to any of us.

I wasn't as good as a friend to Maggie as I wanted to be during that time, mainly because I was looking for my own life preserver. I didn't know how to be a friend to someone who had a terminal disease. Maggie was in and out of treatment, both radiation and chemotherapy, and the Glum Bunch rallied around her, being supportive and loving towards her during this life-threatening situation. Reality hit us in a way we were not prepared for.

One afternoon during her chemotherapy treatment, Suzy and I went to visit Maggie. We'd brought her an adequate supply of trashy magazines and fast food and entered the hospital room while struggling to keep our demeanor bright and optimistic. When I saw her, I wanted to flee from the room and ask the nurse where our friend Maggie was because we must be in the wrong room. Maggie, all one hundred pounds of her, was sitting up in bed wearing her flannel pajamas and watching TV. Her olive skin was ashen while her chestnut brown hair was thinning and falling out. She felt embarrassed and made jokes about it initially, but she knew this wasn't a laughing matter and that it was part of her process to recovery.

Maggie shuffled between Baltimore, where she had been living, and Philadelphia every few weeks for treatments and to also spend time with loved ones. Maggie's mom would have parties at the house for her when she was in town, and we would show up and put-on an air of optimism, but deep down we were frightened for our friend. No one ever talked about her cancer when she was in the room. It was in hushed circles. *How is she doing? She looks good and healthy. She looks like she gained a few pounds.*

Ironically Maggie was able to smoke marijuana openly since she had cancer. We all found this amusing. Her wealthy father became ever present in her life and went around the country to prominent cancer centers to find a clinical trial he could enroll her into. Dana Farber, UCSD Cancer Center, Johns Hopkins and University of Penn, as well as facilities overseas. The grace and optimism that Maggie embodied during her illness was amazing. She never complained about having cancer or having to endure treatments. If she did complain it was only to a chosen few. We were all able to spend as much time as we could with her and cling to faith that she'd beat it.

Two years later towards the end of Maggie's life, she'd been in a coma at the Baltimore Medical Center, and we received contact back home that she might not make it through the week. I struggled with what to do. Go visit her, don't go visit her, call her family and ask them? All of it seemed futile. Suzy, Jenny and I made a decision to drive to Baltimore the next morning to see her. Twenty minutes into the drive to Maryland, the cell phone rang. Maggie had just died. The way I felt at that moment is one I still remember, even today. I didn't cry. I sat, stared out the window and felt a piece of my heart taken from me, and all I was left with was an indescribable sadness. I truly didn't ever think she would die. I wondered if I had gone to church more throughout my life if God would have saved me from the unthinkable death of my cherished friend. I thought she'd get through this and be okay. I thought she was invincible. I thought we all were invincible. One of the biggest regrets in my life was that I didn't get to say goodbye to Maggie, but I have to believe that she is one of my guardian angels watching out for me.

While I sat frozen in the front seat of the car, Suzy teared up, reached over my seat and grabbed for my hand. The feeling and power of touch from someone you love and who understands what you're feeling is unexplainable. A minute later *Brown eyed Girl* played on the radio. That was one of Maggie's songs.

After Maggie died, her family threw a party in celebration of Maggie's life; which was Maggie's dying wish – a party in her honor, an afternoon barbeque. This wasn't your typical burgers and weenies on the grill; that would have been too ordinary for Maggie's family. This was a catered affair with a reggae band to entertain and keep us grooving into the evening. Maggie's mother lived on an estate with a farm house nestled on three acres bordering a well-known Main Line golf course. The estate had a pool, carriage house and a barn that was used to store everything imaginable – except horses.

Maggie touched a lot of people's lives, and a lot of people truly loved Maggie. There were over a hundred people in attendance, Maggie's family, obviously, including all her sisters, her brother and her parents. Julia had flown in from Aspen a few days prior and brought some of her entourage along with her-- those who knew Maggie. Julia kept the festival lively and engaged others in her spirit that afternoon. I had to wonder if she was mourning in private, as I knew most attendees had done at the wake and funeral services. Drinking, of course, was prevalent and in hushed small compartments of the home drugs were evident. This was still a party, regardless of the actual sadness of its origin. Numbing my feelings through this difficult death seemed as basic as writing a eulogy. At the celebration, the opportunity arose for friends and family to speak in tribute to Maggie, and a lot of people participated, Suzy and I in particular. With the help of my mother, we penned a sweet poem that chronicled our friendship with Maggie, and how much she meant to us. It was eloquent and down-to-earth, as Maggie was. It spoke too many, but mainly we knew Maggie would have smiled, if she was present, and we knew she was. I envisioned Maggie smiling from above and jamming to her own celebration with appreciation and peace. The afternoon wound down before dusk, and everyone was given white helium balloons. We wrote a good-bye message to Maggie and released them; mine read, *I love you and I'll miss you*. Simple and True. Watching the mass of pure white balloons lift into the golden sunset sky was a perfect send off to an irreplaceable friend.

January 1990
Main Lion Night Club
Strafford, Pennsylvania

When I first came back from Aspen, I knew I had to get a job and took the easy route by starting to work at my Dad's insurance agency. I hated it. My Dad and I didn't work well together, and my brother had also been working there since graduating from college. He and I didn't get along too well either. I wanted to get back to waitressing. To my Dad's displeasure, I quit working for him and decided to become a full-time waitress at the Main Lion. The Main Lion was a rib-steak-chicken joint that turned into a hopping nightclub after 9:00 P.M. I liked the energy and atmosphere, and most of all I liked the people I worked with. I would work double and triple shifts: lunch, dinner and cocktail. At the end of the night I would mix with the wait staff at closing, and we would drink until 3:00 A.M. and then hit an after hours place, The Devon Bocce Club.

I developed a crush on the nightclub manager, Old Tom. He was thirty-nine, and I was almost twenty-three. He didn't talk that much, but he was always nice to me. We started out as friends, and I would confide in him, and he understood me and listened. He made me feel special. I liked being around him. He wasn't gorgeous, but he had an older, self-confident and sexy quality that made him attractive to me. He had thinning brown hair and steel blue eyes and his face had aged appropriately. Old Tom had been dating a woman closer to his age at this time, and they ran away one weekend and got married. I was a little shocked, but we were just work friends.

After the summer ended, I started working at a real job again. I joined a large corporate company as an Executive Assistant in their Finance department. I continued to see Old Tom at the Devon Bocce Club when I would go out. It was common for me to continue drinking until 5:00 A.M., even though I wasn't working until 2:00 A.M. any longer. Six months into his marriage, Old Tom seemed down and told me about his crumbling marriage. His wife had turned into a selfish money-grubbing bitch that had been cheating on him with a man with more money. One month later she cleaned him out of house and home, literally; he was left with his toothbrush and a dead Ficus.

Old Tom and I ended up talking on the phone virtually every day just to say hi. I would patronize the Main Lion during the week to see how he was doing, and, of course, to have some drinks. He moved on rather quickly after his wife left and seemed genuinely happy she was out of his life. Old Tom was the first guy I knew who actually wanted to know how my day was. That meant a lot. We started spending a good amount of time together after he finished work and would go out for cocktails. Often I'd be too drunk to drive and Old Tom would let me crash at his house, and nothing happened between us for a few weeks.

One morning I awoke at his house and decided to go for it and make the first move. I started kissing him. Instant relationship where Old Tom and I dated for almost two years. He was one of the best lovers I've ever had. He taught me a lot about how to love and how to be loved. He worshipped me and lavished me with love and affection. His age factor was an issue I had difficulty grasping sometimes.

When I introduced him to my Mom she commented, "He's very nice--how old is he again?" I would think for a minute and respond, "I think he's 38, 39 something like that."

For the time I dated Old Tom, my Mom kept asking me the same question, until one day I told her he was 40, and she replied with, "Oh....hmm."

Old Tom was by far one of the best boyfriends I ever had. He took care of me – he did my laundry, cooked meals for me, he helped me with my crossword puzzles, and he held my hand when Maggie died. I treated him the best way I knew how. I broke his heart. I hurt him and left him for someone else.

September 1992
Tap Room USA
Berwyn, Pennsylvania

A man three years younger than I. His name was also Tom, Young Tom. Later on I would realize he was the most brash and insensitive man I'd ever dated. He was a cocaine addict. Old Tom didn't fancy cocaine, and he couldn't tame me any longer. I was restless and missed cocaine. Young Tom pursued me. He called me constantly, followed me around everywhere I went, sought me. I met him when I was out one evening with Old Tom, and he just flirted his tail off. As a woman, I liked the attention and found it very flattering. Young Tom stood at five-ten and was in good physical shape; he had blue eyes and dishwater blond hair with an electric smile. He was charming and sweet in our early days, but his addiction began to shine early on. Within two weeks, I realized that Young Tom was a cocaine dealer. I was actually excited about that, and it became part of the allure. We would date for over two years, and I would get to know him inside and out.

When you drink alcohol and abuse cocaine, a lot your secrets and fears come out, whether or not you really feel them. What you happen to have on your mind just comes out at that time. I shared inner thoughts and feelings with others when I was drunk or high. Getting obliterated became my truth serum. Waking up, or coming to, the next morning I would be flooded with the same feelings--remorse, guilt and panic. *What did I do last night?* More importantly, *what did I say?*

Subconsciously, I wanted desperately to save Young Tom from his evil ways. I didn't know much about his drug dealings at first, but I just knew he always had drugs on him, and I always wanted to do it with him. I was back with my Sexy Bad Boy again. But this time, it was different. I knew what I was doing.

During this time, my parents were coping with their divorce; my brother was married with a baby; and my sister was dating a guy who also was a massive partier and friends with Young Tom. The four of us would hang out together and party on the weekends. It was nice and part of me really liked my life. The other part of me hated my life immensely, but I was so in love with the aspect of being in love with Young Tom and trying to help him that I had trashed my own life in the process. I didn't like who I was and I knew that Young Tom wasn't a nice person. I was constantly making excuses for him and playing down his behavior to everyone else. No one wanted him around, and as a result of the relationship, I began to alienate my family and Suzy. I felt worthless, unattractive and spiteful much of the time.

I had lost all of my weight and looked a zillion times better. That's the thing about addiction and chemical dependency. You live two different lives and always have to put on a show. You know deep down how bad it is, but you rationalize it to yourself over and over and you truly believe that you'll come out the other end okay. I would say to myself time and time again, *"If I could just get Tom clean, then I'll get clean and then we can live a regular life."*

Young Tom's brother and his friends rented a shore house during our second summer together. The house was in Sea Isle City, New Jersey, and they asked us to be members. We did, reluctantly on my part. I was concerned that they'd see our addiction to coke, which we did every weekend during our relationship. I didn't know how we would be able to hide this from everyone.

Young Tom and I would be outside on the deck, drinking and joking around with everyone, and every twenty minutes or so, I'd have to go to the bathroom. I would slip away and go to our room where Young Tom had already cut out lines on a mirror that he had hid under the bed. I would sometimes go in and change my outfit after I snorted a line, just so it would look good to everyone else, and I could keep them at bay. Some of the members in the shore house were also buying blow from Young Tom. I rationalized it that way. I just didn't want his brothers and their girlfriends to find out. That is where I was protective and cautious. I actually had most of them fooled too. I became very close with Young Tom's family. They became my family.

I had shunned my family because Young Tom wasn't always extended a loving invitation. I would have Sunday dinners with his family and not attend my own family functions. I would spend Christmas morning with them and barely see my family that afternoon. This drove a wedge between me and my family. My father and I got into a messy disagreement and didn't speak for three months over the Christmas holiday because of Young Tom. My dad didn't like him at all, and he wanted me to stop dating him. My father had a gut feeling that Young Tom was full of shit. I made a decision to walk away from my father and stay with Young Tom.

I didn't want anyone to know what our relationship was really like though. I thought I knew what I was doing, especially since I had already dated another coke dealer. However, I didn't understand the magnitude of Young Tom's addiction. He was a maniac and although he never physically abused me, he mentally abused me every day of our relationship, and I believed most of what he said. He got agitated frequently and would pick a fight with me if I didn't say what he wanted to hear. I had to agree with him about every decision he made, or he would get pissed off at me. I was a feisty thing and didn't give in too easily. I felt fighting was part of a relationship; that's what I saw growing up, and it seemed normal to me, even though I knew our fighting wasn't healthy.

Nothing was ever resolved and our disdain for one another grew stronger. We'd make up and be okay for a day or two, but that never lasted. Some of our fighting was in front of other people too. Sometimes his parents and brothers would scold him about it. His mother nicknamed us *The Bickerson's*.

My addiction was in full force, but I can't blame any of this on Young Tom. I chose to snort as much coke as I possibly could, to drink as much booze as I could, and to also stay in a seriously unhealthy relationship. No one was holding a gun to my head. I tried to leave him several times, but he wouldn't let me, and I couldn't make a clean break. I caught him cheating on me. Shocking! Another coke dealer who cheated on me!

I finally made him make a decision, give up her or give up coke. He looked me right in the eye and said, "I choose coke....and her."

Our break-up was difficult for me to get over quickly, because as tyrannical as he was, I did care for him. And I didn't want to give up my gratis coke.

After the breakup, though, I knew I couldn't blame my mate selections for the choices I was making in life. I had to stop placing blame on everyone else and be an adult to make my own choices matter–which they did for the next four years. Yes, indeed.

Chapter 11

November 1994
828 Columbia Avenue
Lancaster, Pennsylvania

After the Tom stretch, I spent a lot of time with my closest Glum Bunch friend Suzy, and her boyfriend, Hank. Hank had a close friend from high school in Lancaster County, Pennsylvania, where he grew up. His name was Dean, and he was the closest thing I've ever had to a soul mate. I had known Dean for years but we always had a significant other in tow, and normally I never gave him more than a second glance. He wasn't drop dead gorgeous, but his smile showed that he cared, and he was appealing with his dancing green eyes and hair which mingled premature gray in with the brown.

One evening while I was at Suzy and Hank's apartment for dinner, they shared with me that Dean was on his way down from Lancaster for the weekend. I was ambivalent about it but knew it'd be a good evening to go out and drink and be amongst friends. Dean showed up and maybe it was the way he looked at me or the fact that I was looking for anyone that would offer me special attention, but after many drinks at the local tavern down the street from my apartment, he walked me home, and he slept over. It was a little awkward, as most one night stands are, but this didn't feel like that. It felt different, but I didn't want to try to foresee anything more than just us having a good time and keeping it between friends.

Future-tripping is a problem I have when I start dating someone. Within one week of dating them, I envision picking out china patterns and reciting his last name after "Mrs." Mrs. What Guy I'm dating at the time. Dean left in the morning and went back to Suzy's apartment. The three of them had plans the next day. He told Suzy at the end of the day that he wanted my number. He called me the following day, and thus our courtship ensued, the Lenox pattern already chosen.

Five months later in April 1995, I quit my job in Wayne, and moved an hour away to the wholesome Amish town of Lancaster County to live with Dean. We were very much in love and had a healthy relationship. It was the coming together of two souls, and I told my Mom, *He's the one.* I felt it two weeks into dating Dean. We liked the same music, shared the same views, had the same friends, and yearned for a future together in suburbia. We believed in and supported each other, and our life together felt domesticated and certain. I would cook and clean for us, he would spent time in the yard, we would rent movies during the week, and on the weekends go out with friends in Lancaster or drive to Valley Forge to be with my family or Suzy and Hank. We vacationed, camping in West Virginia, riding bikes on the island of Nantucket, visiting Kimberly in San Francisco, spending time with his college friends in Rehobeth Beach and New York, and we also went to visit friends I still had in Colorado. Dean became part of the Carr clan, and my family made him feel like one of us. For the first time in years, I enjoyed my life and was able to share it with someone else. I felt I had found what I had been searching for and it was with Dean. I like to refer to this period as the calm before the storm.

Dean and I had a blissful first year in Lancaster. I became acclimated to the landscape of horse buggies and shoo fly pie. Dean had just purchased an old house in downtown which needed a lot of restoration. He spent a lot of time renovating the house, a thankless job that took years and one I barely got involved in. It was too messy and complicated for me. Realistically, I was too lazy to put my sweat into a home I wasn't thrilled with in the first place. He purchased it right before we started dating, and I tried to become a gardener and plant flowers when I could, but mainly I sat around and cooked, shopped, did the laundry, drank and smoked pot.

Dean was a daily pot smoker, which made it easy for me to smoke it, but I never really liked it that much. I wasn't much of a pothead because when I smoked pot, I would sit on the couch, eat a bag of Dorito's and watch any John Hughes movie I could find. *The Breakfast Club* was a classic, and I related to it so well. Pot made make me very paranoid and goofy, but it was a motivator for Dean. I was amazed at how much he could accomplish when he was high. I had stopped using cocaine on a regular basis and was only drinking four or five nights a week. This was real progress.

Nonetheless living with Dean was an adjustment for me. If I didn't get my way, which was minimal, I would get pissed. I was usually drunk or hung over when this occurred, and the term *Bitch on wheels* was one that seemed to fit. Dean had a huge fear of abandonment from his childhood. His mother had left when he was six years old and didn't come home for over a week. This was something that followed him into adulthood. I didn't know about Dean's fear until one morning when we got into a nasty fight. I threatened to move out, which I did every so often. I had packed up a bag and told him I was leaving, but I left only for a few hours to go shopping at the outlets. I came back and found him upset, sitting on the kitchen floor. I felt awful, and he told me about his abandonment fear. I never tried that stunt again. I was always pushing his buttons to try and scheme and get what I wanted. I just wanted to get married.

I thought marriage was the answer and it would offer me a true sense of security and love, something I sorely lacked. Having a husband would complete me in my mind. I wanted the wedding, the dress, the party, the honeymoon and everything else that went along with it. Or so I thought. I was never comfortable with whom I was and being alone was not an option for me. Almost every time Dean and I would go out for a special night, I would conjure up how he was going to propose to me and where the sparkling diamond ring would be. Is it under the dessert plate? In the champagne glass? Is the waiter going to bring it out on a silver platter? Where is it? I never found it. I let myself down every time and then I would pick a fight with him. Gee, I wonder why he didn't want to marry me.

During our second year, I got laid off from my administrative job in Lancaster and started looking for a new position. I started networking with my old contacts back in Wayne looking for a senior level administrative role. The salaries were at least $10,000 higher than they were in Lancaster. I decided that I would look in the Valley Forge area and commute back and forth. I was hoping that Dean and I, in the near future, would get engaged. This would make him want to leave Lancaster and come back to reality, living along the Main Line. Which is kind of an oxymoron when you think about it? The Main Line is a compilation of scenic towns for the privileged suburbanites of Philadelphia.

Eventually, I secured a position as an Office Manager for a small business owner in Strafford, Pennsylvania. I commuted from

Lancaster to Strafford every day, two hours round trip through rain, snow and sleet. I did this for over a year until it simply got to be tiresome. I finally moved in with Jenny to be closer to work, and Dean and I would see each other every Wednesday night and every weekend. One of us would drive up on Wednesday after work, spend the night and then leave on Thursday morning. By Friday evening we were together again. It was challenging not living together after two years of cohabiting. Having freedom away from Dean soon became enticing. I started drinking more during the week, and my old insidious friend was knocking on my door again and would visit me for a couple nights here and there–but not at a level that I felt it was a problem.

I thought my drug use was recreational. I didn't need it daily to function, nor did I sell myself out for it. Financially I was strapped and had dug myself into debt, but I convinced myself it wasn't because of my drinking and drugs. I would rationalize it each and every time, yet in the back shelf of my brain, where I filed away the seedy dark truths, I knew exactly why I was in the financial, mental and emotional state I was in. It was because I had a problem. But who would I tell? They would have found me out and realized that I was a fraud and a loser. I had to keep my dark private life, private. I hid my recreational drug use from Dean and thus the secrets started. Never a good thing in a relationship.

I had intensified the pressure to get married, and Dean kept saying *wait six more months*. I believed him. I wanted to get married so I wouldn't get to that place of discontentment where I would sabotage our relationship. In all of my relationships I felt that I had fucked them up solely on my own. I knew I wasn't really that bad of a mate, though, and consciously started to try and make our relationship work. However, after failing one too many times, I would tell myself I was worthless, and that no one would want to be with me. Hell, I didn't even want to be with me.

In September of 1997, Dean and I planned a weeklong vacation to Nantucket. I had planned the whole trip—transportation to the island, reservations at the quaint bed and breakfast, the bicycle rentals, dinner reservations, and I even brought some wine. What a great travel companion I was. I earned the nickname Nanner the Planner from my sister since I was constantly planning everything in my life. On Mondays, I would start planning where to go for Wednesday and Thursday nights, calling and e-mailing people to see who was around, where we could go and what time to meet. During the afternoons at work, I would think about what wine to buy on my way home from work. Should I go with my normal two bottle magnum of merlot? That would mean I'd drink the whole thing, so if I bought a decent single bottle of Kendall Jackson or Beringer, then I would only drink the one bottle. But then I'd want a second bottle for tomorrow night and on and on and on I would scheme, except I would rarely drink just one bottle of wine a night. I would always open up the second bottle for *just one more glass*. Inevitably I would have to go to the neighborhood bar or run to the store to get a third bottle, depending upon how tired I was. The planning of social activities went simultaneously with my drinking. I went through phases of what I drank, which had started with beer in Junior High and High School. In my late teens, I'd discovered Vodka and started making concoctions with different mixers and juices and finally settled on my standard, Absolut on the rocks with a splash of water and lemon or splash of cranberry juice. I discovered Wine in the late 1980's during the trendy Chardonnay explosion. Easy to drink. Light, fresh, crisp and it seemed so harmless.

Dean and I arrived at Nantucket by way of Hyannis Port on a small six-seater putter plane, and if we could survive that twenty-minute excursion, we could survive anything. This would be the proposal trip. I felt it, I wanted it. The princess attitude emerged and my thoughts were racing to when he would propose. During a bike ride and picnic through Sconset? At a candlelight romantic dinner in a restaurant on Straight Wharf? If Jesus had walked into our B&B room and told me that Dean wasn't going to propose, I would have assumed he was a fraud and crucified him myself. The pressure was on. Jenny was getting very serious with her new boyfriend, and a lot of our friends had married the previous summer. The first three days of our vacation was glorious. We lounged, ate, drank, smoked, rode our bikes all over the island and enjoyed each other. Our fourth night there, we went to a bar after dinner. The name of the bar was *Brothers*. Why I remember that and no other place in town, I don't know for sure, but I guess because people remember where they were at fatal moments, like 9/11. I had been drinking since 4:00 P.M. that afternoon when our Bed and Breakfast hosted the daily happy hour. We were sitting at a table listening to the acoustic band, and they were playing a song I really liked. I don't remember which one, James Taylor or Billy Joel, some sappy song I knew Dean just hated. I was annoyed the marriage discussion had not been brought up during our vacation yet. I didn't want to jinx the night by asking him about it, yet again, but being drunk, I pushed it. When I approached the subject, he was pissed. I clearly wasn't going to get my proposal. He pursed his lips, furrowed his brow, held his head in his hands, and sighed—all his typical mannerisms showing how bothered he was.

He looked straight at me then and said, "Nance, I am not ready to get married, and right now is not the time to discuss this."

I remember gulping down my beer and fending off tears. "I thought you were going to propose on our trip. Are you telling me that you're not?"

Dean wiped his brow with his hankie. "No, I'm not. I'm still not ready yet."

All I heard was that he didn't want to marry me. Period. Now, we had been together almost three years, and at the ripe age of thirty, I was ready to settle down. As I looked at Dean, I started to cry.

"I can't fucking believe this. We have been together for almost three years. I am the best thing that has ever happened to you, and in six months I'll be the best thing that will happen to someone else."

I got up from the table, left the bar and started walking away. Dean came out after me a couple minutes later and just stood outside. He didn't follow me or try to speak to me. He just stood there smoking his cigarette. I proceeded to walk into another bar and order a drink. I drank my cocktail and then left, walking alone back to our B&B.

One of the things about Dean that drove me to the verge of insanity was that he never got openly upset with me. He always maintained his composure. Whereas I was yelling, screaming and barking callous remarks. Being raised in a somewhat hostile environment, fighting was the way to solve all problems and disagreements. That's just how it was; there was no reasoning or compromising. Children learn what they live. I was never in a relationship where there was no fighting. I would pick fights with boyfriends just to express frustrations in my everyday life. My father had expressed his disdain through anger to everyone around him and I learned that was the way to be heard in order to get what I wanted -- control and manipulation. As sick as it sounds, I got off on anger and rage. However, I didn't realize then how much fury I had burning a hole in me. Drinking and drugs fueled that fire and relieved me of my inner fury. It was my fix for my fix.

When I arrived at our B&B and entered into our room, Dean was sitting by the window smoking a joint. I walked in, still pissed, and looked at him and thought, *Fucking fight back, god damn it, and don't be such a fucking pussy.* I wanted him to express to me what he was thinking and that meant yell back at me. Be a man and express your anger. But most people didn't harbor the anger I did. I found that out years later. I'd also learned to swallow my surface anger.

Dean and I made up a few minutes later after I apologized to him, saying it would never happen again. It didn't for another twelve months. I clearly didn't have the Greek Goddess of Love working for me in my favor.

In August 1998, Jenny got engaged and was to be married in October. My relationship with Dean was hitting some bumps. I was upset about us still not being engaged, and I had a pretty loose summer. I spent a number of weekends in Avalon with a girlfriend of mine and ended up cheating on Dean. I kept my infidelity from him, but started pulling away from him. At the end of the summer, I started traveling to San Diego for work. I became very entrenched in my career and flourished within the company I was working for. The company was an Executive Search Firm.

My boss wanted to open a second office in San Diego and appointed me project manager, handing me the task of opening an office. I had to be accountable and control my partying ways, as I usually could when an important career assignment was involved. I spent five weeks traveling back and forth from Philadelphia to La Jolla, California. San Diego, California was and is one of the most picturesque and lovely places I had ever seen—in my limited experience. If you like sunshine, the ocean, and a free-floating lifestyle, San Diego is your next home. Driving along the Pacific Coast Highway, I couldn't help but be mystified that I was able to spend time in this coastal town. I couldn't believe people, families no less, actually lived here. I loved every visit to San Diego and couldn't wait to go back.

I soon started thinking that I didn't want to be with Dean anymore. I didn't want to wait four years for the love of my life to figure out if he really wanted to marry me or not. If he truly wanted to be with me, he would have asked by now. I wanted to explore the San Diego paradise and not look back. I wanted more excitement, more adventures, more time to enjoy life and party.

I came back home after another business trip to San Diego mainly because Jenny was getting married that weekend. I was her maid of honor, *always a bridesmaid never the bride*. I had been in five other weddings up to that point and was always wondering if and when my wedding day would happen. That saying always seemed to wiggle its way into my head at every wedding I was in or attended. However, this bride was my baby sister, and I couldn't have been more excited about her nuptials. Dean, of course, was my date.

I was very uninterested in him at that point and had come to the decision that I was going to end our relationship. I wanted nothing to do with him that night. I was stressed out about the wedding and being the maid of honor. I was also jealous. I was supposed to be getting married first, not my sister. I wanted what I couldn't have.

The wedding was a joyous occasion. I drank, did my normal amount of cocaine, and then couldn't wait to get the hell outta there. At 4:00 A.M., Dean and I came home from the post-wedding party, where we had an hour long conversation in which I broke up with him. It was difficult and taxing, and I was completely wasted and not sure I was making the right decision. At 5:00 A.M., I thought my thinking was clear and sharp. Dean asked me if I had been faithful to him during our last months.

My truth serum was pumping through my veins. I told him I wasn't and was very sorry for what I had done. We sat there crying and just sitting on my stairwell for a few minutes, and then he stood up, gathered his belongings and opened the front door slowly. He looked back at me with tears in his eyes and said that he had been ring shopping for me.

I didn't believe him. I wanted to hook him up to a lie detector test, flip the switch and watch him squirm.

Needless to say I struggled with this decision for a few years. I wish I could have done things differently. That's the problem with alcoholics; we want what we want, when we want it. No prisoners. After I had time to sober up and realize what I had done, my normal feelings of remorse and guilt crept back in. I wanted Dean back in my life as it was, comfortable. Even if it meant sacrificing my own wants and wishes to get married. Desperate to get Dean back, I made a mix tape of our songs, which alone is sophomoric, and sent it to him with a pride-forsaken letter fraught with apologies. He pulled away and our communication waned. I felt like I had wasted four years of my life with someone I thought I could rely on to love me unconditionally.

Not wanting to take responsibility for my own actions of infidelity and harm to our relationship, I catapulted quickly into my usual vat of alcohol, drugs and men. My lifeboat hadn't arrived yet. I finally decided in early 1999 that I was going to move to San Diego in late summer. I needed a change of scenery and wanted to be around new people. People that didn't know me.

In order to get over the hurt and pain of the break-up, I had found another suitor to entertain me for the next few months in Philly. A classic Irish drunk and cocaine addict. After my four year hiatus, I had a lot of time to make up for. Irish Drunk was a humorist and a genuinely sweet guy with floppy dark hair and tall at six-two. But he was also wrapped up in his addictions. He couldn't follow through with anything, nor could he ever commit to doing anything. I couldn't ask him on a Thursday if we could meet up with friends the following Friday. He was a very spontaneous person, and Nanner the Planner couldn't make any plans. I put all of my planning energies into my relocation to San Diego and researched where I wanted to live, how to find a roommate and mapped out my cross-country drive to California. I still had a few months to enjoy spring and summer before my trek out West. I made the best of them.

May 1999
Electric Factory Concert Venue
Philadelphia, Pennsylvania

Keep on Trucking. I had been following the *Grateful Dead*, as much I could afford to, since 1986. I wasn't a true Dead Head since I bathed on a daily basis and didn't live in a VW bus selling veggie burrito's to support my marijuana and LSD habit. I did, however, like to go to their concerts along the East Coast; New York, Philadelphia, Virginia, Washington D.C and anywhere else they played. It was always a weekend event consisting of tailgating, drinking, tripping on LSD and listening to timeless and amazing music. Suzy and I had a huge crush on the bass player, Bob Weir. Bobby would take the microphone to sing and we would scream up to him that we wanted to bear his children. We had class.

After Jerry (Garcia) died in 1995, I replaced my Dead shows with concerts of Bob Weir's band, *Ratdog*, later called *The Other Ones and the Dead*. Howard, an aging, balding and overweight hippie was friends with a colleague of mine. We now had an inside track to the inner circle of Ratdog. We were going to be able to meet the band before the show. I could hardly contain my excitement. I was going to meet my crush Bobby and this was sure to be the highlight of my entire existence.

As we waited patiently outside the decaying concert hall, I felt a little stupid. There were eight or nine of us waiting for Bobby to show up, and we looked like Pavlov's dogs awaiting the bell that brought our reward. Twenty-five minutes later an ominous black Range Rover pulled up to the rear stage door and four people got out. There was Bobby. I was nervous as hell and couldn't stop staring at him. He looked spaced out, but I wasn't surprised to see that. Here was a man who was a member of one of the most influential bands of all time and who participated in Ken Kesey's infamous acid test. He was God to a lot of people. He quickly took Jerry's place after his passing, and now he was standing dead center in front of me.

Meandering out of the car, Bobby looked worn and sleepy, with unruly hair, he wore a stretched out faded blue t-shirt and baggy jeans. He resembled what an aging rock star should look like – an icon who had spent the past thirty years drinking, drugging and living life in a hurried world pleasing the masses. Bobby inched his way over to us, and

Howard introduced my colleague and me to Bobby. I gingerly shook Bobby's hand as I made eye contact with him and told him how great it was to meet him. He didn't hold eye contact with me at all and was looking over my shoulder. I was disappointed. Didn't he know I was one of his biggest fans? Didn't he want to get to know me better? Ha. Bobby soon became more attractive to me as a rock star singing on stage than he was as a real person. He wasn't present in the moment as a real person to me and seemed more like a mirage of who I thought he should be inside a human body. But, he'd obviously met hundreds of thousands of groupies in his time who also didn't think of him as a real person, and this tiny connection with me was nothing. Selfish, as I was, I thought I would at least get a smile out of him.

Howard supplied us with All Access VIP passes, and we were able to follow the crew onto the stage and be part of the real inner circle. Yeah Baby! I noticed a man carrying instruments and cables across the stage. Cable Boy was very appealing with his shoulder length dark hair, brown puppy dog eyes and a dazzling smile. That's all I needed to see.

During the concert, Howard took me to the sound board, where I was granted access to listen to the band directly through the headphones. I was also granted access to the green room, which had a full bar and a buffet. After the rollicking concert, I went back to the green room and hung out with the band and the crew. I was eyeing up Cable Boy and getting the same reception back. Drinking a beer and making small talk with the band members, I weaved my way over to Bobby to listen to his conversation and see if he had any words of wisdom to extend to me.

I didn't get a glance my way, so I bee-lined back to the bar and grabbed another beer. I was feeling antsy and decided to take a seat on the plush green velvet couch. I plopped down on the couch with a sigh, and within minutes Bobby came over and sat next to me. Gulp. I was sitting on a couch next to Bob Weir. What did I do to get so lucky? I wanted to call Dean and tell him what he had left behind. A full-fledged ex-Grateful Dead hippie. I had a key to the inner circle -- and I was somebody – and he missed out. A waft of smoke was coming from my left side, as a joint was being passed around the room.

Finally! I was wondering when the drugs would come out. When the joint passed over to Bobby, I was nervous and had made a conscious decision not to drink too much or smoke a lot of pot that evening. I had the wherewithal to know I wanted to be aware of the events of the evening and not be in a black out. That idea had vanished about two songs into the first set, however. Bobby took a toke and then haphazardly passed it over to me.

Are you fucking kidding me? Bobby Weir is passing a joint to me? This is far-out. I was mildly shaking when I grabbed the joint and took a long hard puff on it. I was sharing Bobby's saliva. I was as high as one could be. Soon after, the inner circle party was transported to Bobby's suite at the Four Seasons Hotel in Center City. Howard had decided to go home, but I'd be damned if I was going to leave this open invitation. Cable Boy had invited me, and I could hardly believe my great luck. The festivities continued on in a palatial suite with other roadies and groupies.

Giddy, I walked into the suite only to find the band crew sitting around a coffee table drinking and smoking pot. The suite had leather couches with the perfect upscale hotel room décor--muted greens and beiges accentuated by a navy blue to give the room a calming effect. This room was not calm, by any standard. The group was smoking pot and bottles of champagne, beer and wine littered the dark mahogany coffee table, strewn everywhere; some half full, others empty. I drank it all in and was soon drinking what was available to me – anything I wanted. *Let the games begin.*

Bobby was conversing with a band member in the next room where four hookers were also in attendance, making small talk, or whatever you'd like to call it, with the other band members. I was dumfounded that call girls were in attendance, but being naïve is a prime characteristic of mine.

Hot Cable Boy made his way over to me and started asking me if I liked the show. He asked me a lot of questions about myself. Where did I live? What did I do? Was I married?

At first I thought he was very interested. I later realized he wanted to make sure I wouldn't try to follow him on the road and become a nuisance to him while he toured. He wanted to make sure I was a real person with a real life. We were heavily flirting, and I knew where this was going. He was very sweet and nice and just kept smiling at me. How high was he, I wondered. It was 2:00 A.M., and my newfound friend offered to get me a taxi home in the morning. A man with a plan. I found my match. Moments later, Cable Boy suggested we move the party to his room. I was smitten with him and excited to join, although I couldn't help but wonder how many other women he had invited to his room. Hundreds, I supposed, but I didn't care.

We had a very nice time that evening and in the morning I felt like Julia Roberts in *Pretty Women*. My life was one cinema show after another. There I was sitting on a Queen Anne chair in a fluffy hotel bathrobe with everything from the breakfast room service menu ordered for me. Cable Boy and I talked for a while. He told me I could keep the robe. I felt awkward. He then gave me his phone number, along with two tickets and VIP passes to the concert in Atlantic City the next night. I jetted back home in the taxi and was dizzy with my prior night's experience. I went to Atlantic City that night and took a friend of my brother's, who is a huge Dead Head and indebted to me still. Nothing ever happened with Cable Boy and me again, and through the years when I attended *Ratdog* concerts, either in Pennsylvania or San Diego, I would seek him out, and he would remember me. He normally gave me VIP passes and show tickets for other concerts. Nice to make friends with boys in the band.

In late summer *The Other Ones* were playing at the Tweeter Center in Camden, N.J. It was a beautiful July afternoon and almost immediately I was smoking pot and trying to drink as much as I could before I had to enter the stadium and pay five dollars for a beer. After the concert I befriended some people, in particular a guy who was throwing a party on his Winnebago bus. I had lost my tribe of friends and ended up on the party bus in the parking lot with my hippie *subject* for the evening.

I don't know how much time had passed, but the Winnebago started moving. I had asked everyone where we were going.

"To the party!" they screamed.

I didn't care where we were going and thought what the hell; I'll deal with this when I deal with this. That's how I handled every situation when I was drinking. I didn't care where I'd end up, nor did I try to anticipate what the consequences would be. The next morning I woke up next to someone I didn't know, and I was over 150 miles away from home. It was pathetic and humiliating. It was a holiday weekend, July Fourth, and all the car rental companies were closed. I had to take a taxi back home. $275.00 later, it became the most expensive taxi ride I ever had. The driver appeared to be ninety-five years old. This probably wasn't the first time he'd seen someone in cut-off jean shorts, a tie-dyed t-shirt and matted hair that needed a ride. Clearly my life was unmanageable, but I wouldn't admit it. This became one of those funny stories to tell people, and it still is, to some extent. But knowing that I put my life in danger in a situation where I could have been raped or even murdered, lingered with me for a while. I was lucky to be alive and safe. Another bullet dodged.   But how long would my luck hold? I needed this fresh start, this new life ahead of me in San Diego. But first, a few visits along the way….

Chapter 12

August 1999
Heading West

Slamming the trunk of my Honda Accord with the last of my personal belongings inside, I took out my carefully planned itinerary map, courtesy of the Rand McNally website, and drove away from home. I was embarking on a road trip that would start a new phase of my life, the unknown.

Departing from Philadelphia, I drove eleven hours to Cincinnati, where I spent two days with an old colleague. Helen and I had worked together as Executive Assistants a few years prior. We were fifteen years apart in age, but had formed a special friendship. She was like an aunt to me, and I could confide in her about anything. Almost. She was someone I didn't drink with, nor did she know about my drug habit, and I would never divulge that to her. I felt guilty not sharing all of my lifestyle with her, but felt that she couldn't comprehend the way I lived my life. I was ashamed of it myself, and to press it upon her would make me feel even worse. I would only tell her enough surface information to keep her involved in my life. I liked having friends who weren't aware of my double life. It gave me the illusion that I really wasn't that bad of a drunk or drug addict, and that my wild life-style would wind down soon.

We spent our two days getting pedicures, walking around the stimulating town of Cincinnati, eating at fine restaurants and casually drinking wine, which was torture for me. I couldn't wait until my next destination. Vail.

When I lived in Aspen, I bunked with a waitress that I had worked with at the Hotel Jerome. Carly was bubbly and blond, five years younger than I, and liked to drink the way I did. We had both fled Aspen at the same time seven years earlier and remained close friends. She moved around a little and settled in Vail where she worked as a massage therapist. I was anxious to see her since it had been a couple of years—and I was eager to have some real drinks.

I made a promise to myself that I wouldn't drink while driving cross-country, which wouldn't be smart since I needed to focus on my driving and reaching my destination. I couldn't risk a car accident or a

DUI now, though I'd often driven under the influence or hungover.   I was amazed at how many DUIs I didn't receive, especially the next morning on my drives home from wherever I had passed out the night before, or worse yet, driving to work. Numerous mornings I would drive to work hungover, and I'd feel paranoid and nervous when other cars would zip past me. Drinking and driving on this trip couldn't be allowed. I gripped the wheel with two hands at all times to concentrate better.

I never felt like that when I drove while drinking. I felt like the conqueror and thought my driving was actually better. They say for every DUI you get, you have driven drunk 200 times, at least! At that point, I'd been pulled over numerous other times while I was drinking and luckily, I was let go.

Weaving through the Rocky Mountains, I felt a presence of pure joy overwhelm me with the potential of a new life on the horizon. I sensed that I could achieve anything in California. The Promised Land awaited me. I arrived at Carly's condo just in time for happy hour where the fragrant aspen trees reminded me of my days in Aspen. Carefree. I spent three days with Carly. We ate Mexican food, drank *cerveza* from the bottle and made pitchers of margaritas. I met her group of friends, and they became my fast friends. A successful visit by any standard. Carly now lives in Michigan with her husband and two children, living the suburban lifestyle. She settled down when she got married, and like other friends of mine, she grew up. I still had a lot of growing up to do.

Scottsdale, Arizona. I love the desert. Kimberly and I spent our thirtieth birthdays there two years ago, and I really fell in love with the mountains, the vast landscape of cacti and the golden evening skies. Nightfall in Arizona is fresh and magical, with stars glistening in the limitless sky. For five days, I visited one of my oldest and dearest friends from back home. I needed the five days on this visit. It would be a doozy.

Bob Collazo and I met when we were in ninth grade. Because of his last name, he was nicknamed "Oz." We were friends all through high school, but never spent a lot of time together. We ran around with the same group, and when our friends went off to college, he and I found ourselves stuck at home. To dilute the impact of my lifestyle and its seedy cocaine companions, I would spend time with Oz. We became close friends and would spend our time together, driving through Valley Forge Park, smoking pot and pontificating about life and what our futures had in store for us.

This was the start of a treasured friendship and one I still have today. Italian by heritage, Bob's features of dark hair and brooding eyes gave him a mysterious and sexy persona. Slight in stature, he took care of his body and was proud of his toned appearance. Bob had been living in Scottsdale with a couple friends from back home, but he also had new acquaintances for me to meet.

I pulled into the driveway of his rented house, a gorgeous four-bedroom home, landscaped with cacti and colorful ground cover. There was a large back patio and a pool with a waterfall coming off the Jacuzzi. This was a nice pad. Oz had four roommates, a southern boy he befriended from Tennessee, two girls, and a close buddy from Boston. Beantown Boy—a tall Irish kid from the South Side. He sported blond spiky hair with ice-water blue eyes, the party animal of the crew. I could tell as soon as I entered the front door that he would be able to keep up with me. He walked over to me with a cocktail in hand and a cigarette in the other.

"Whoa Ozzie, is this is your friend from Philly?" he asked as I set down my luggage.

I looked over at Oz who raised his eyes to me. "Yup, this is Nance. Be on your best behavior with her."

As soon as Oz said that, it was evident that Beantown Boy and I would become fast friends. There was an instant attraction. No sooner than I came out of the bathroom after my eleven hour road trip, I had a vodka cocktail in my hand. Finally, I could relax and be myself. I could drink with Carly, but being around Oz always gave me a sense of extra security and comfort. I spent the next five days drinking, lying out by the pool, getting acclimated with Scottsdale and its surroundings, and snorting blow with Beantown Boy, and whoever else was at the house.

Oz went through an experimental phase with cocaine, but he never liked it. Smoking weed and having a couple beers kept him satisfied. Oz and his friends became an important part of my social life when I moved to California. Beantown Boy and I started an affair during my visit, and this continued for the next couple of years when I would visit Arizona, or when he and Oz would drive over to San Diego to spend time with me. My Arizona pit stop was a great foray into my San Diego independence, as it set the stage for my newfound philosophy of living life on my own terms. I wasn't accountable to anyone -- except me. I had no family or close friends to monitor what I was doing. This would become a curse to me later on. So here I am. 3,000 miles from home. Doing whatever I wanted.

August 1999
7595 Charmant Drive
La Jolla, California

Driving into San Diego, California was one of the most liberating experiences I had ever felt. It seemed as if I had an eight leaf clover in my back-pocket, and great things were going to happen to me. I was a mere thirty-two years old, but I felt like I was eighteen. I had spent the previous ten days driving cross country with eyes wide open.

I knew two people when I moved to San Diego, and one of them was my new roommate whom I'd met through a roommate referral service on line. I wanted to find someone normal; however, *normal* to me wasn't *normal* to most people. Cynthia seemed like a nice ordinary person, and she was. Born and raised in Porterville, California, a suburb outside of Bakersfield, she was petite at five-four, and sported a blond bob haircut and had a cherubic smile. She was a smart girl and had earned her Master's degree in Psychology from the University of Illinois in Chicago. She had also just left her husband of two years, after finding out that he was gay. She was twenty-eight years old and had barely touched alcohol—a notion that I couldn't fathom.

She didn't like to drink when she came home from work, and she barely drank when we'd go out. I thought she was a goody-goody, but she just wasn't an alcoholic. We would go out downtown to go dancing, something I could only do when drunk, but we would flirt with guys and sometimes she would even kiss them. Cynthia smoked her first joint with me one night, and we spent the evening bull-shitting about guys and how stupid they were. Typical female conversation. Two months after living together, Cynthia started dating our neighbor, and they soon became inseparable. Her new boyfriend was in the Navy. They married a year later and now reside in Annapolis.

I made a life for myself in my new home. I decided to settle in La Jolla in the University Town Centre area. This section of La Jolla is home to UCSD students, singles, young couples, and many businessmen on expatriate assignments. La Jolla is also the Life Sciences hub for San Diego, the industry that I work in. My office was in La Jolla, and I wanted to be in the middle of everything. It was a turning point in my career where I was being trained to become a recruiter for senior level executives in the biotechnology community.

This was a huge learning experience for me which set the foundation for a career where I began to surpass my own expectations. This role gave me the opportunity to form relationships with prospective candidates and clients and to free me from my administrative career that was no longer challenging me. I'm amazed at how I was able to easily grasp the concepts and responsibilities of this newfound role within my company. It was also amazing that I sustained my partying lifestyle and still carried out my position in a professional manner. There were plenty of nights, however, where I wouldn't make it to bed that night and then strolled into the office hung-over. Usually my boss would know what I had done, shake his head at me, and tell me to take it easy.

I was what's called a "high-functioning" alcoholic. I could sustain, for the most part, my lifestyle in order to accommodate my career. Being able to make my lifestyle seem to involve only social drinking was highly important to me, and I thought that if others around me saw that since I could keep my career intact, I didn't have a real problem. However, I knew better. Most alcoholics are highly functional and are able to achieve financial and career success; it is one of our traits – live, work and play hard.

I wasn't able to maintain this lifestyle on my budget for more than a few months, and then I started going to payday loan offices to borrow funds until my next payday. I continued to operate in this manner for a number of years, justifying this way of living because it was so expensive to live in San Diego. At least, that's what I kept telling myself. The shame and embarrassment I felt walking into the money store was always there, but I forged ahead and kept telling myself I wasn't that bad. I looked okay on the outside, and that was all that mattered to me. I would walk into the money store with my

Prada purse, Coach Wallet, driving up in my fully loaded Honda Accord. Big hat, no cattle. That's what my Dad calls people who look like they uphold a certain standard of living on the outside, but have no assets and are in debt. I should have moved to Texas.

While Cynthia was busy spending all of her time with her Navy man, I had to make do with learning the lay of the land, or shall we say beach. The other person I knew was my sometime boyfriend, who was the head chef and restaurant owner of a four-star French restaurant. He introduced me to red wine, a beverage I thought I wouldn't enjoy as it was too dark and bitter for me. Red wine soon became my best companion and beverage of choice. I became engrossed in red wine varietals until I quit drinking. I couldn't get enough of it and held onto current health reports that it was beneficial. Although, health experts suggested one glass a day, I preferred one bottle per day and used this as another excuse to drink daily and reassure myself that I didn't have a problem.

Chef and I dated briefly, but it turned into more of a friendship. I would frequent his restaurant a few times during the week to drink and nosh on delicious gourmet fare. I made friends with the wait staff and would occasionally accompany these young twenty-somethings out to see live music and shoot pool. I soon knew where the local watering holes were and ventured there on my own.

On one such evening, I ended up going to a campy outdoor Mexican café called En Fuego, located on the Pacific Coast Highway, also called 101. The locals would go there for happy hour. I happened to saunter in one autumn night, pretending to be waiting for Cynthia. This is something that I did frequently. I made believe that I was waiting for someone to drink with, when in fact I just wanted to go out and drink, regardless of whether someone was meeting me or not. I kept checking my watch and cell phone to make it look good.

It was a slow night with only about seven patrons at the bar. I noticed a flirty couple in their young forties across the bar from me. They were laughing and kissing and acting like teenagers. There was a tall blond surfer type to their right who would interject conversation with them every few minutes and seemed like he knew them. Blondie looked like he was in his late thirties and was your predictable California bad boy--smirky grin and deep piercing blue eyes like the Pacific. After my second gold margarita, Blondie called me over.

"Hey why don't you join us? Your friend isn't coming. You need to have a drink with us."

I smiled with my East Coast grin and said, "Thanks, but she'll be here soon."

Blondie walked over and sat next to me. "C'mon, there's hardly anyone here, it's not like he won't find you."

I laughed and noticed that he was much cuter up close. "How do you know it's a he?"

Blondie was intrigued. "Even better. Come over and join us, and we'll all have fun."

After living only two months in San Diego, I had found someone who partied the same as I did, in excess. Blondie and I spent four months together, off and on. He took me to Rosarito Beach, Mexico, where in another country anything goes. I remember leaving my underwear in a Mexican bar bathroom and not even thinking twice about it. Tequila and cocaine can make you do crazy things. Blondie turned out to be a short-lived fun time who wanted nothing to do with you when the alcohol and cocaine wore off. He was a thirty-eight-year-old party boy, barely divorced and understandably didn't want a full-time girlfriend or commitment.

Before Blondie and I stopped dating, he invited me to a Super Bowl party which his roommate Vinnie also attended. Ironically, Vinnie was from Lancaster, and immediately he and I struck up a friendship. We had a Philly connection. GO EAGLES! Vinnie was with one of his best buddies, Matty. Vinnie and Matty were quite a pair. They liked their whiskey, their cocaine and their cigarettes. It suited me fine. I was heavily into my Vodka and red wine phase at this time. I remember having a great time at the Super Bowl party with the highlight being 7:00 P.M. ending, West Coast time. We still had plenty of time to keep the party going. I also liked the fact that football started early in California. I didn't feel guilty opening up a bottle of beer at 10:00 A.M., since it was acceptable and the bars would be packed by 9:30 in anticipation of the first 1:00 P.M. EST game.

When Blondie stopped calling me, I started hanging out with Vinnie and Matty. It was kind of odd at first, since Vinnie lived with Blondie. But Blondie was always conveniently out of town. On many a night, the three of us would hang out, play cards, drink and party with *Joey* until the wee hours of the morning. Joey became our code name that we gave cocaine; it sounded better, not so taboo and easier to say out in public. It sounded cool.

"Hey, when are we going to meet Joey?"

"Want to see Joey after these drinks? Okay, let's boogie out of here."

"Is Joey coming to meet us tonight?"

I would sometimes leave Vinnie's apartment at 5:00 A.M. and go into work at 8:30 A.M. This weekday behavior stopped after a few weeks of feeling like dog shit. Serious partying was now only meant for Thursday, Friday and Saturday nights. At the time, I wasn't attracted to either Vinnie or Matty, and I could completely be myself around them. It was great as I felt like one of the guys. We could barely pay for gas, but we always had enough money for booze and Joey. The three of us were living hand to mouth in prestigious La Jolla, California, and if you looked at us, you would have thought we weren't living beyond our means. Oh, but I knew we were.

Chapter 13

Christmas 1999
1111 Chambria Court
Phoenixville, Pennsylvania

I went back to Philly in 1999 for
Christmas and to spend New Year's Eve 2000
with my family and friends: the new
Millennium, Y2K and the hoopla that was to be
associated with it. I was excited to see
everyone after living in San Diego for all of
four months; it seemed like years. I stayed with
Jenny and her husband and Tyler, my eight-
month-old nephew and godson. For my visit
home over the Holiday, my company had
rented me a car, since I was also going to be
spending a week training some new staff in
our Philadelphia office. I couldn't wait to go
out and rip up my old home town with Suzy
and Hank. I flew into Philadelphia at 6:30
P.M., and with no time to waste in order to go
out and have a good time, I had a drink in my
hand by 8:00 that evening. Yet I was heading
for a buried land mine. That night changed my
life.

I had plans to meet Suzy and Hank for
dinner in Malvern at a local restaurant. Suzy

was in an anxious mood and it seemed that she had some exciting news to tell me. Two drinks into dinner, she blurted out, "Dean is engaged!"

I slammed my drink. How could this be? I just moved away and now he's engaged? We only broke up a year ago. The guy I'd been waiting on for four years was engaged? He and his ex-sweetheart from college had found each other again. How romantic. Yippee for him! Three days after I left Philadelphia to drive cross country to San Diego, Dean became engaged to his ex-college sweetheart. What a wuss. He had to wait for me to leave the State of Pennsylvania to get engaged. Dean's fiancée was financially secure as her Grandfather was a pioneer in medicine, inventing the world's first cough drop. Big whoop. Dean had to hire a lawyer just to decipher the pre-nup.

I wanted to get up and vomit.

My family and Suzy didn't tell me before I flew back home for the holidays because they wanted to spare me from the despair and sadness they knew I would feel. At least in telling me at home, they could comfort me.

I was staring at my drink and looked over to Suzy and Hank and just teared up and left the table. I remember running to the bathroom to really cry and twist out the knot in my stomach, and luckily for me I had brought Joey with me.   I felt like someone had thrown me out of speeding car, and I was skidding along, heels over ass. I was in complete shock. I hadn't even known how much I wasn't over the hurt and loss of losing him and the future that should have been ours, in addition to being upset that he had been able to move on in his life. My life had changed enormously, but not my feelings for him.

I felt like Sally in the romantic comedy, *When Harry met Sally*. Sally's sitting on her bed crying as she just found out her ex-boyfriend got engaged. She says to Harry, "The thing is he wanted to get married, he just didn't want to marry me." How did my life quotes wind up in blockbuster movies?

The night got ugly, and two bars and dozens of drinks later, I drove my rental car home to my sister's house. Or I tried to.

I drove about a mile out of Malvern, and gosh darn it; I knocked over a trash can while sideswiping a curb. Seconds later I was pulled over for suspicion of driving under the influence. Angry at being pulled over, I felt justified since I was suffering the emotional trauma of Dean's engagement. Wasn't there some clause in the constitution or penal code where we could just forget about this? Couldn't we just call this a Mulligan?

No such luck. I blew a .18, which I thought was respectable, and was arrested for DUI. My Pennsylvania license was suspended, and I would have to take a partial DUI course in California

This arrest caused no major problems for me, and no one in my family made any reference to the fact that this could be an issue for me. No one commented on my out-of-control lifestyle. My father handled the mess for me. One of his friends became my lawyer. Dad helped me pay the fine, and he commented to me, "Your number was up. Everyone drives drunk. You just got caught this time around."

I felt that I had no problem controlling my alcohol, none whatsoever. I got my butt back to San Diego, and applied for a California driver's license to cover up the Pennsylvania suspension, and it worked. I was back in business, confident of getting over this obstacle and continuing my way of life, unaware that my lack of control over alcohol and drugs was escalating.

I remember attending the California DUI education classes, all six of them, which were torture. The first thing our instructor said to us was that 50% of us would be back in the next five years for our second DUI. I thought no way, not me. I'll be more careful the next time around, and I will never drive drunk again. Never. I also didn't pay attention to anything in that class. I zoned out and would go out every night after DUI School and get drunk. It seemed like the thing to do given that the class was on Wednesday nights, which was always a night for me to go out and drink. Whether or not I had to attend a DUI class that night, it made no difference to me.

May 2000
La Regencia Apartments
La Jolla, California

In early spring 2000, my nine month lease with Cynthia was soon to end. I had to find a new place to live and fast. I ended up finding a roommate through *The Reader*, a local San Diego newspaper. It's not too smart to find any kind of a roommate in a free local newspaper, as I was about to learn. I had found Cynthia through a service, where you pay money to meet nice normal people--people who aren't throwing Ecstasy parties till 2:00 P.M. on a Sunday afternoon, (with the party having started the evening before).

My new digs were great. My new roommate was your average twenty-seven-year-old dude from Orange County, enjoying the So Cal scene. OC Dude was a Marketing Manager for an emerging dot.com company in San Diego. Our roommate situation was fine at first and I was still partying like a rock star whenever possible.

OC Dude had a new group of people he met at the afterhour's club scene in and around San Diego. He was easily influenced, willing and vulnerable, just what they needed. He learned how to snort coke and take Ecstasy and then bring the party home! After months of living in party hell—even for me—if you can believe that, I moved out. I already had my Ecstasy phase in my early twenties. I was much happier drinking and scoring Joey.

Shortly before I made my decision to go AWOL on OC Dude, he had invited me to go out with him and his friends. I had no major plans and thought, if anything it would be an interesting evening, and I was always one to experiment with a new crowd of people and atmosphere. OC Dude and his gang had decided to attend a Rave at Club Velvet, which was located inside the Del Mar racetrack. It catered to the suave and sophisticated party goers of Del Mar. The younger girls that evening were dressed in tanks and mini-skirts purchased from the trendy Forever 21 store at the mall, whereas I wore a classy black suede mini skirt, teamed with high heeled black boots and a red halter top. Everyone was dancing and rolling on Ecstasy, drinking bottled water when I arrived. I wasn't sure I wanted to roll on E and was hoping we could just score some Joey, but when I found out that was unattainable, I said, sure why not try E. I hadn't done it in years, and I had heard that the new E was sometimes laced with heroin, a drug that I never wanted to try. I took one hit and waited for it to take effect. Thirty minutes later it had hit, and I found my boy toy for the evening, a twenty-six-year-year old professional surfer. Surfer Boy was darling, shorter than most, with a washboard stomach. He resembled Matt Damon and was one of the boys I actually *do* remember. He took me to an after-hours house party at 3:00 A.M. after Velvet had closed.

The party was held at a large stone mansion in La Costa where the host looked to be fifty years old and reminded me of Dennis Hopper as an aging eccentric hippie in the movie *Blue Velvet*. Everyone everywhere reminded me of famous people; actors, rock stars, politicians, socialites—they all had a place in my world, and I felt it was easier to relate to people that way. It made them seem less real and less approachable, but I could also live in the fantasy of who I wanted them to be. Connecting with real and true people was not easy for me to do, and the more fantasy that was involved, the more I felt like I was in control.

Old Hippie Dude had an enormous back yard with a hot tub, a brick lined patio, lap pool and cabana. I remember walking into the kitchen soon after we got there and found a half-dozen people sitting around a huge mirror snorting lines. They looked at me and simply offered me the straw. I grabbed it quicker than you can say Joey. When I looked at the powdery substance, however, I realized it was a light shade of blue. This wasn't coke, it was Ecstasy. I was already rolling and feeling no pain, and decided why not?

It turned out to be one of my worst nightmares. I was pretty sure there was something more laced into this Ecstasy. Upon snorting it, the rapid rush was unexpected and an hour later I started feeling queasy. I found Surfer Boy and told him I thought we should leave. We had taken a taxi to the party, so I didn't have my car with me. Not smart. Never be at a party without an exit strategy.

Surfer Boy told me that he was leaving with his friends, and they couldn't take me home as they were going north and wouldn't go south to La Jolla. Bastard Boy ditched me. How dare he? I hoped he got eaten by a great white when he caught his next gnarly wave. I was distraught; I knew no one at this party, but knew I needed to get home. Plus, I had no money, so I couldn't call a taxi.

With no money or friends at the party, I decided to go outside to see who was leaving and if I could hitch a ride to La Jolla. Someone had to live south of La Costa. I walked out onto the long driveway of the mansion and parked on the street was a Greyhound bus. I was pretty tweaked at this point. The sun was starting to rise, but I didn't think I was seeing things. Why would a bus be here?

I approached the driver who was just revving it up. "Excuse me sir, where are you going?"

The haggard bus driver looked annoyed that he even had to drive the bus, let alone deal with a stray party girl at 5:00 A.M. in the morning. "I am taking the people that rented this bus back to Pacific Beach."

Wow people had actually rented a bus to drive them around that night. Smart crowd. "Oh, right. I think I'm supposed to be on this bus, but I live in UTC. Can you maybe drop me off before you head into PB?"

The party guests started filtering out of the mansion and were making their way up the driveway to load onto the bus.

"I'm not sure those folks are going to be too pleased that we have to make a pit stop in La Jolla."

At this point I knew I needed to start begging. This was my last chance. If I couldn't get on this bus, I'd be stuck in the house with Dennis Hopper. "Please, please, please drop me off in UTC. You can just take me to the closest street from I-5. It's just right off the freeway. Please, I'd be so grateful. I have no other way home."

The driver looked at me and sighed, "Well you should have thought of that when you got to the party. But yeah, hop on, I'll do it."

I had never been so elated to get on a Greyhound. As the bus started driving South on the 5, I knew the partiers on the bus were ready to go home and rest up. This would not go over well when the bus took a detour to UTC. That is the last thing that anyone wants when they are worn out coming down from a night of partying. Driving south on the 5 from La Costa, the driver slowed down and exited at La Jolla Village Drive. I sat and stared out the window, hoping no one would notice. People stopped talking and noticed we were exiting, questioning the bus driver, who wasn't responding. They started shouting.

"Hey what is this?"

"Where are we going?"

I felt I had to make a stance and stood up. "I'm really sorry, everyone. This nice driver is going to drop off me off near my apartment since I have no other way home. I apologize, but thank you for your understanding." I was so proud of myself. What a great explanation. I took my seat, hoping to hear no backlash.

No one seemed to agree with me, and the shouting continued. "Are you fucking kidding me? This is what we paid for, Jesus Christ." People started booing and throwing trash at me.

It was so humiliating, almost as humiliating as walking the four blocks back to my apartment in my rave outfit, not something you'd expect to see at 6:00 A.M. on the streets of La Jolla.

I decided I had to get out of the UTC area and move to Del Mar. UTC had bad karma. It wasn't me. The justifications and rationalizations just kept on coming.

I left UTC for reasons beyond the rave incident, however. I wanted to get away from the Blondie and OC Dude fiascos. Better yet, I wanted another geographic. This would be my third move in less than thirteen months. I ended up, of course, not learning my lesson from the living scenarios with the OC Dude. I found a new roommate, again from the *The Reader*, this time, a twenty-two-year-old girl from Mexico City, a student at USD, who was studying psychology. Later on, this would become quite ironic, considering she was involved in psycho-therapy and taking every imaginable anti-depressant and anti-anxiety drug on the market. So much for self-help.

This nesting period started with Marlena and a new environment. In the early months, it was great living with Marlena, or as I lovingly called her, Salma, she reminded me of Salma Hayek. Initially, we got along and had similar attitudes that begged to be reckoned with. We drank, we smoked, we had men issues, and we liked to say *fuck* a lot. I learned some Español from her. Additionally, she had living room and kitchen furniture, something I surely didn't have, and the apartment was in Del Mar—two more bonus points, as I was already hanging out a lot with my Super Bowl party friend Matty.

After a few months, I had cooled off being around Vinnie because of the Blondie situation, but Matty and I started doing things together without Vinnie, actually, just drinking and meeting Joey together. Matty also lived in Del Mar and introduced me to a lot of party friends on the Del Mar circuit.

Another fresh start. Fingers crossed this one would work out.

Chapter 14

January 2001
Caminito El Rincon
Del Mar, California

    2001 New Year's Eve, the night I befriended Kristen. Kristen was five feet, nine with light brown hair, a solid girl, but not overweight. She excelled in track during her high school years and kept her athletic physique. Kristen hailed from a dysfunctional Italian – Irish household, much like my own, and was ten years younger than I. If I'd been sober when I met her, I am sure we would have never become close friends. What brought us together was our palette for wine and drugs. She soon became my partying counterpart for a number of years.

    Going out socially during the week was always on Monday's and Wednesday's. Monday Night Football was a reason to start the week off right and Wednesday nights were my DUI class nights and also the mid-week hump, Hump Day. Each of those nights I would meet Matty at a local bar and drink. He was bartending then, and his schedule was Thursday, Friday, Saturday and Sunday. It worked out quite well for me, since I had just met some new Del Mar friends, compliments of Matty, who knew *everyone* in Del Mar. Matty had spent the last nine years of his life there and worked in almost every major restaurant and bar in town.

I met a girl one evening through Matty named Sandy. Sandy had a lot of problems. She was clearly an alcoholic and an addict, but in a soft nice way, and I initially thought she had her life together. However, it didn't take long for me to realize that she had very poor self-esteem and constantly needed to be the center of attention. She never stopped talking, and she was always sad or depressed. She asked me if I would spend New Year's Eve with her, and since Matty had to work, I agreed. At the last minute she invited her friend Kristen along, and I quickly said, "Yes, please do!" I was thinking, great, a buffer.

Earlier in the week, I'd found out about Sandy's two failed suicide attempts in the past five months, and I wasn't even sure I should be hanging out with her. Three girls in a crowd are better than two. It turned out that New Year's was a night spent suppressing Sandy from drinking and snorting too much while she kept whining about how she wanted a boyfriend. Kristen and I started our friendship that night based on our mutual disdain for Sandy. It grew from there.

Conversely, my roommate situation with Marlena wasn't offering any friendship. By summer I had seen Marlena go out with three or four different men, each one giving her more heartbreak than the last. I was also spending more time with Matty, Kristen, and her boyfriend, Bryan. The four of us would burrow at my apartment before heading out for the evening. After a few weeks, it became evident that Marlena felt uncomfortable with me having company over, and she became quite vocal about it in front of my guests. There was awkwardness in the air.

I personally liked Marlena, but she thought we partied and drank too much and that I wasn't available to her enough. I wasn't her friend, I was her roommate. I didn't know I had to be available to her as a friend. She was over ten years my junior, and we had different life schedules. The fact that I wanted to party and have fun was my business. The tension grew each month, and to top it off, she didn't know how to clean or cook. She was brought up in Mexico City as the daughter of a doctor and had maids handle the basics for her. I'm a bit of a neat freak that can't stand dirty messes. Eventually it worked out okay as our lives had different time tables.

There were a couple of nights where either she or Matty drank too much, and the claws would come out. I couldn't wait for our lease to end in December. By Fall I was already starting to look for a new apartment.

U-Haul knew me on a first name basis and I decided to ring them up again, for yet, another move.

By this time, moving every few months didn't seem abnormal. It made sense. Lease is up, you move. When I told Marlena I didn't want to renew the lease, she agreed.

It was during the early spring of 2001 that I started having romantic feelings for Matty, a shock to me as much as I think it was for him. I really liked him as a friend, and we enjoyed each other's company. Mainly we could talk and communicate, and we liked the same sad sappy songs, and of course, liked to drink and drug. We shared the same outlook and could relate to each other's lives before we knew each other. We were brought up in the same kind of toxic family environment; divorce, drinking and various madcap scenes, although we were both very close with our respective families. The friendship was comfortable, and we enjoyed living along the coast, especially since Matty owned a Harley, and we would ride through the coastal towns of San Diego and frequently drive up the coast to Laguna Beach for the weekend. Sporadically, we would go to LA and visit his friends there for weekends of heavy drinking and drugging. We barely slept when we visited LA; his friends partied the same way we did, hard and fast. However, all of this took money, which he rarely had, and I became the roaming ATM. I was making $50,000 per year, which kept us living the freewheeling lifestyle we had, but it was extremely taxing on me.

In addition to going to payday loan stores, I started going to a pawn shop in Pacific Beach pawning gold and diamond jewelry that I had received as gifts through the years. More embarrassment and humiliation.

My friend Sara, who I had made friends with through Oz in Scottsdale, came to visit me one weekend, and Matty suggested we come into Scalini's, the restaurant where he was bartending, and have a couple of cocktails. Scalini's was an upper crust Italian restaurant situated at the foot of the Polo fields in Del

Mar. It catered to the older and affluent Rancho Santa Fe and Del Mar crowd. I knew I would usually be one of the younger patrons when I frequented Scalini's. Sara and I entered the lounge, dressed to impress, and found it crowded with tanned, eager men in their fifties in addition to ageless women, adorned with designer jewelry and outfitted in haute couture. When Matty saw us enter and wiggle up to the bar, he quickly poured each of us a glass of Opus One. I proceeded to make the proper introductions.

As soon as Matty walked away, Sara smiled over at me and commented, "He's cute ..and he's got a nice ass too"

I was actually surprised. I never thought of Matty that way at all, ever. I responded to Sara, "Are you serious? Really? I've never seen that."

All of a sudden it hit me--he was cute, and he did have a nice ass, and he was one of my best friends. I fell in love with Matty at that moment. Needless to say it took me a while to deal with this bombshell news and even longer to let him know my true feelings. Within a couple of months I had communicated to him, verbally and in letter form, my true feelings. He didn't reciprocate.

He explained that it wasn't a disinterest on his part, but that he wanted his life to be stable. Who was stable at this point? All we did was drink and snort blow. The reality was that he was still getting over his heart-wrenching break-up with his prior girlfriend last year. He wasn't ready to get involved with anyone again, but he was flattered.

For the time being, Matty and I remained as we were, a kiss occurring between us intermittently. It was torture for me, and in order for me to move on and maybe make Matty jealous, I started seeing someone else. One evening Matty and I were having dinner at one of our regular restaurants. We were eating at the bar, and I noticed a handsome young man. He wore smart spectacles and looked intelligent with boyish good looks. Stud #73, Spectacle Boy. I started talking and slipped him my business card.

He called me a few days later, and quickly, a fondness for one another developed. Spec Boy was very much in touch with who he was and could talk for hours on the phone with me about anything. I enjoyed the attention he showed me, but was still pining for Matty. Spec Boy would call me frequently during the day, usually when I was with

201

Matty. I could sense it was annoying Matty, but he'd had his chance with me. I started to like Spec Boy in a superficial way as I was trying to block out Matty. I knew that I was playing Spec Boy to get to Matty, and it worked.

Six weeks into dating Spec Boy, Matty sat down with me and told me that he wanted to date me exclusively, and asked if we could be together. I didn't hesitate one bit, called Spec Boy the next day, and broke it off. I was ecstatic to finally be with Matty because of the strong feelings I had for him. I thought Matty hung the moon and stars; he was the ying to my yang.

January 2002
Torrey Bluff Drive
Del Mar, California

I decided I wanted to get my own apartment after moving out of the Condo with Marlena. I knew it would cost a little more money, but I figured I'd be able to make it work, somehow. I moved into a beautiful one bedroom apartment that had a clubhouse, pool, tennis courts, washer/dryer, dishwasher, and full amenities. It was across the street from the neighborhood shopping center in Del Mar. It was bliss to have my own place, finally no roommates. The only furniture I owned was my bedroom set, so we used beach chairs and an empty box as our coffee table for the first few weeks.

Within a month my father had bought me a couch, my mother had bought me a TV, and I purchased knick-knacks from local garage sales. I was in a good spot. I had my Matty, my own place, my friends, and I was living in San Diego. One week later, Matty moved in too.

My happiness didn't last long.

Matty drank every day while wanting to have Joey over most nights, and he wasn't motivated to work. On the weekends this worked out great for us, but during the week it was hard for me to keep my career going and maintain any sense of well-being. I would arrive home from work to find my apartment cleaned, laundry done and dinner simmering on the stove, and of course, Matty drinking. I would drive home from work and say to myself, *I'm not going to drink tonight, no matter how much Matty has been drinking. I won't drink. I can say no.*

That never happened. I would walk in the door; find him drinking and raring to go. I would be pissed at him—only for a minute though. Soon I would drink my *one glass of wine*, which led to a full bottle and then Joey and more drinking. Bravo, another repeat performance.

I remember during one of those specific occasions, I woke up the next morning and told Matty I was going to quit drinking and using because I didn't want to live that lifestyle anymore. He scoffed. I quit—for two days. I just kept coming back for more encores, couldn't stop, no matter how many times I told myself I could. Matty and I used to joke together that he was *Mr. Mom*. The sad part was we had no children or pets to take care of.

Matty had stopped working altogether and was drinking every day and seeing Joey as much as he could. I was supporting both of us, paying rent, utilities, food, telephone, and, of course, all the party materials. Matty had lost his bartending job at Scalini and would bartend elsewhere here and there, but it was evident that as much as we cared for each other, our life together was unraveling. Matty felt guilty for not working and knew his life was shit, and that he was causing me anguish.

We fought almost daily, and I would tell him to leave, and he would for a couple days, but he would come back, and we would drink and drug together to make ourselves feel better.

In June, Matty decided to move to Indiana, where his Mother and Step-father lived, to start a new life and to run away from the temptation of the sunny and glorious California life. He wanted to run away from the demons.

I was very depressed after Matty moved away, and my drinking was now daily. I was doing coke at least three nights a week alone or with Kristen. I had kept the party going, but I was lonely, and it got even lonelier in the darkness of my apartment, wishing that I too could just run away. I needed a diversion.

Enter Stud #76. One evening of carousing around the town of Del Mar by myself, I met a twenty-eight-year-old cutie patootie. Stud #76 seemed to like me and gave me attention, of course he was drunk—I could have been a kitchen utensil. Cutie Patootie worked for his Father's company, soon to be his company, drove a Lexus, and lived in a posh condominium in Del Mar. Stud #76 resembled George Clooney—to me he did. He had dark brown eyes, cropped hair and a robust physique.

We dated off and on for a few months. In the beginning, we would talk almost every day; see each other during the weekends, and usually one evening during the week. He traveled a lot for work and had a very busy life with his family, social and work obligations, and we liked each other's company. I realized it was mostly on his terms though. He wanted to see me only when it was convenient for him. There was real no relationship to our relationship. I personally wanted more, and he sensed it, and we both started pulling back from one another.

Stud #76 ended up becoming a good friend, but he is not the kind of person you can have a deep discussion with, unless of course you're drunk and doing Joey. Another person that likes Joey. I figured out that most of my friends in San Diego were friends with Joey who was so easy to find in Del Mar. He hung out at McDonald's, Von's, the Shell gas station and popular bars.

You always knew where to find Joey-- and other drugs, easier than going to buy gas. You called a number on a beeper, left your phone number, then the dealer would call you back, normally a Mexican that barely spoke English, and he would tell you where to meet him. It was always in public crowded places—which made me nervous, but I thought the Mexicans had a good reason for it. They never got arrested, or at least not during the few years that I was using their services. It was a perfect user-friendly operation, and I was very thankful for it.

Unable to have Stud #76 fill my void; I felt the only friend I had now was my bottle of wine and frequent visits with Joey. I started to isolate myself and only wanted to drink alone at home. To rationalize my drinking at home alone, I would run to Trader Joe's after work and buy a few bottles of wine, along with crackers, cheese-spread dips, and a bouquet of flowers. Envisioning that others would see I was hosting a small cocktail party, or going home to my loving husband, I would switch cashiers each visit in order not to be recognized. I bet the cashiers never even gave it a second glance, but I was paranoid that everyone would know I was a sad lonely girl who drank alone. I needed to do something drastic to get out of my skin, some new experience.

Joining friends one afternoon at the Del Mar Racetrack in late summer, I met someone who was nice, attractive and engaging. While placing a bet for my third trifecta race of the day, a man, who seemed to be in his late thirties, smiled and started asking me questions on how to bet. I didn't know how to discern a horse from a pony let alone how to bet on the horses. Smiling back, I commented to him that I just picked the horse by the name. "Oh, I bet by the name of the horse. For this race I'm wagering my bet on *Furious Frankie.* He seems like a good one to place my money on. I really don't have a system that works. I just wing it and hope for the best."

From the start, I was attracted to him and felt that I could lasso him in with my charm. He was shorter than most men I dated at 5'9, but looked like a soap opera star to me nonetheless. Radiant smile, almost perfect nose and medium brown hair, to describe him without a visual doesn't do him justice.

He smiled at me and asked if I wanted to grab a drink. Magic words. "Sure, sounds good. I'll take a Corona."
He ordered my beer and then a Diet Coke for himself. Hmmm. Maybe he's being responsible as the designated driver for his

friends. Mildy shocked, I looked at him while squirting my lime into the icy cold Corona.

"So, you don't drink?" I realized I was being nosy, but I had never met anyone that didn't drink, unless they were pregnant.

"Naw, I haven't had a drink in over three years. I got sick of the hang-overs. But, please feel free to, don't let me stop you."

My initial reaction: *Perfect, I'll have a designated driver.* I really liked this guy but him not drinking was too challenging for me and I felt like a loser all the time, because I couldn't stop drinking.

Sober Man and I lasted two months. One evening, after I had polished off a bottle of wine with dinner, he got up and told me that I drank too much, and he wasn't able to baby sit me anymore.

Jenny had given birth to twins three months earlier. I barely knew my two-year-old-godson, let alone my new nephews. I was stricken with extreme homesickness, and by July, I'd informed my company that I wanted to spend October, November and December back East to be with my family. They agreed to let me work from a satellite location and keep me on the payroll.

In October, I put all of my stuff in storage, packed up my car and drove cross country, yet again. It was almost three years to the date that I'd arrived in San Diego. On the road again. Yet another Geographic. The road trip was again filled with visits along the way.

In Scottsdale, I visited my life-long friends, Oz and Sara. I had spent a lot of time in Arizona while I lived in California, and it was great to make a pit stop on my way back East. One incident that occurred while I was in Arizona is one that still sticks with me.

We will not regret the past, nor wish to shut the door on it. This lesson was still to be learned at this point. Even now I sometimes wish the past would drift away, though. Of course it doesn't. If I forget how bad things were in my past and how unmanageable my life was, I will drink, so I have to keep my memories of the past fresh, not matter how humiliating.

The incident was after a *long* night of partying with Oz and his friend Beantown Boy, the same guy I'd slept with sporadically during my visits to Arizona and on his visits to San Diego. Matty was gone, and I'd acted out in any way I could with other men after he left for Indiana. At 6:00 A.M., Beantown Boy and I decided to take his jet-fueled Kawasaki motorcycle out for a spin. This was after Oz had told me at least four times that night *not* to go riding with Beantown boy. I swore to him I wouldn't. However, it seemed like a really great idea to go watch sunrise in the desert. Beantown Boy and I were racing down a deserted road at ninety-five miles per hour in an obscure part of Scottsdale called Troon when I heard the sirens. Police sirens. Fuck.

I informed Beantown Boy that the Fuzz was on our tail, and he proceeded to speed up, the theory being that if you drive over a hundred on a motorcycle, the cops stop chasing you. Well, this didn't occur with us, and minutes later, Beantown Boy and I were pulled over. The cop was less than amused, considering he had been following us for the better part of a mile. It turned out that Beantown Boy's bike was not registered, and deemed illegal and Beantown Boy was taken away and arrested for a non-registered vehicle, speeding and DUI. This was Beantown Boy's third DUI, his first one on his motorcycle.

The cops hauled Beantown Boy away to the station house, and they were no help to me in finding a ride back to Oz's house. It was nearing 8:00 A.M., and and I found myself in the hot desert vicinity of Troon. I didn't have a cell phone or any money. I had the tow truck driver, who carted the cycle away, drive me around Troon to see if any of the homes looked familiar. All the homes had the same familiar look, brown stucco with terracotta roofs and gravel-strewn cactus landscapes. Even if they did have any distinguishing features, I had no brain cells left to figure out what they would have been. I was numb from the episode, and I just wanted to go home, wherever that was.

The tow truck driver deposited me at a local convenience store where I spent the next six hours basking in the Arizona sun and sitting on the curb until Oz came to get me. The clerk at the mini-market took pity on me and fed me fountain sodas and pretzels. I called my sister and Suzy collect to relay to them another stupid incident that I found myself in. Clearly, my life was manageable and this happened to a lot of people, right? No one that I knew of, though.

On the road again. I made a pit-stop in Indiana to spend a few days with Matty. It was comforting to see him and hold him and kiss him. We ended up getting a hotel room, meeting Joey, and drinking the weekend away. Some things just didn't change.

Chapter 15

October 2002
Kramer House
Phoenixville, Pennsylvania

Picture this. I arrived at Jenny's home, or rather my new home for the next few months, and entered the kitchen. My 2 year old nephew, Tyler, sat in his booster seat, eating something that looked soggy and unpalatable, and next to him were my eight-month-old twin nephews in their high chairs sucking on their bottles while throwing Cheerios. It was kiddie mayhem; food all over the place, the children crying, screaming, laughing, who could tell at this point? All the while Jenny and my brother, Bobby, were having a casual conversation.

"Hey Guys." I entered, sensing a mix of excitement and horror.

"Nan, welcome home, so good to see you!" Jenny said, hugging and kissing me. As I looked around the kitchen, I was mortified. What had I left behind, and what did I now enter? Kiddie hell.

I immediately poured a glass of wine and took a load off. This was going to be an adventure. I was more concerned for them, though, not me. I was only the Aunt.   My brain quickly started working on a new social plan: Get out as much as you can while you're living here.

Coming back home after being a resident of California for the past three years left me a little lost. All of my friends were now married and entrenched in their suburban lives. Falling back into our pseudo party days clearly wasn't doable.

Within five days, however, I had found a guy who partied just as much as I did, and he adored me. Resembling Vin Diesel, he was ten years my junior, barely employed and lived in the attic of his grandmother's decrepit home. He was going places.

One of the problems, among others, was that I never wanted anyone to know we were together when out publicly. This is where my warped sense of who I was became such an illusion. I thought I had it together as I looked okay on the outside, but inside I felt like a failure in all areas of my life. After a while, when Vin and I were out, it didn't really matter where we were as the only places we went were dive bars. Vin Boy let me be myself around him. He also let me walk all over him, which I regularly did.

In the beginning of our relationship, I told him that we would just casually date. Vin would call me three or four times each day, and depending upon what other social engagements I had for that evening, I would determine whether or not to call him back or blow him off. I, of course, started dating other men. Or should I say boys, not men.

Enter stud #89: a seemingly pre-pubescent college student. He was twenty-three years old and stood at Six-two, with dark brown messy hair, blue eyes and chiseled features. He looked like Benico Del Toro. The Hollywood comparisons just never stopped. Suzy and I had gone out one Saturday evening, and I decided we needed to extend the fun and hit the local after hour's club in Wayne. The Italian American Club. A great place to meet quality men at 2:00 A.M.: bartenders who are just finishing work, college students who are ready to roar, and your classic drunks and drug addicts—everyone who just can't seem to get enough after last call. Me included.

Benico walked in, and I tagged him immediately. That's how I operated. I would

215

set my sights on a guy I thought I could attain and try my darnedest to do so. I loved that feeling and it became a game of cat and mouse for me in those last few years of my fanatical party life. Most of the time the wranglers I would lasso in didn't stick. Normally because whatever lives we had at the time were inspired by drinking. These guys were just as drunk as I was and were also wondering the next morning, "What the hell did I do last night?" Not a good start to a loving and intimate relationship, especially for someone who wanted to get married. I had pretty much abandoned the whole marriage notion though at this point, in favor of my entrenched philosophy: Party 'til I drop.

I felt refreshed and renewed after moving back home and started going out five nights a week and making new single friends, all younger than I, with one exception. Benico did come back with me to my sister's house one evening, where I wasn't surprised that breakfast wasn't served to us in the morning by Jenny. Jenny had now tired of shaking her head at me and sighing with displeasure as to what, or whom, I was doing in my spare time. I drove Benico home to a large colonial that he shared with six brothers and sisters and his parents. I'd probably met his parents at a Dead Show ten years earlier and shared a joint.

He was young and I was just filling the same void that alcohol and coke poured into. Benico was finishing up his doctorate in philosophy at Villanova and worked for a non-profit organization during the day. We had a peculiar romance that didn't last long. I can't remember all of the men during this time, just that I had the rotation going on by then, my revolving love interests during that era, quite a merry-go- round. Besides Vin Boy, I had a few other suitors that I don't remember too clearly. I saw them out around town quite a bit though, which became very embarrassing when I was with one guy and ran into another.

My black-outs were regular then, and I had to call whoever I was with the night before to find out what I did and said the prior night. Gosh, I hated that. I was so uncontrollable when I drank, I didn't care about anything except drinking and scoring some Joey. Vin Boy had a local connection where we could get Joey every Friday night–a huge relief.

After living with my sister and her family for five months and completely falling in love with my nephews, I decided it was time for another geographic and moving in with my

217

Mother seemed to make sense to me. I ended up staying in Valley Forge for a while. Why not? I had no sizeable bills and no major responsibilities. I was working a few hours a week for my company in San Diego; they didn't know exactly how much I was actually working. Being a recruiter, I had to produce a couple of candidates each week for the searches I was working on, and our client's needs had slowed down after the Holidays.

The laidback life was working for me, and it was nice to be near my family and friends again, and as usual, it was all about me and what I wanted and when I wanted it. True alcoholic selfish thinking.

In early 2003 I was recruited to an International Search Firm. The recruiter got recruited. The firm had five offices in the U.S and five offices overseas. They had one in Newport Beach, California and if I proved myself with the corporate office in Princeton, N.J., I would get a chance to move back to California if I wanted to. I wasn't sure where I wanted to live, so I decided to stay in Valley Forge for the time being and stay with family until I had to make a final decision.

I moved into my Mother's three bedroom townhouse until I could figure out my next home. Stay in Pennsylvania or go back to California? This decision would have to be made soon as I didn't know how long I would be able to live with my Mom, seeing as I hadn't lived with her since I was eighteen. I hoped she still made bunny-shaped pancakes for breakfast.

March 2003
Mom's House
Chesterbrook, Pennsylvania

I walked into my mother's house that early spring Saturday afternoon holding my Hefty bags of clothes and belongings, and I felt like I had walked into the Golden Door Spa. There was classical music playing, her house was clean, and I could smell a sweet aroma emanating from the kitchen. And my mother was drinking some wine. This was quite a switch from the Kramer House of boys and chaos. Don't get me wrong, I truly loved my sister and her family, but this was such a peaceful environment to walk into. I felt calm and relaxed. For about three hours. Then my mother became my mother.

"Honey bunch, what are you doing tomorrow night for dinner?"

I was thirty-six years old and my mother still called me "honey bunch."

Oh gosh, here we go. The planning of evening dinners. This might be a welcome situation for most people, but for me it wasn't. I was in such shame with how I was living my life, I didn't want to sit down and have dinner

220

with my mother and converse. The one positive was that dinner would always include wine. I was always very conscious of how much wine my mother had. I had to make sure I would get at least three glasses. Two with dinner and one to take upstairs to go freshen up with. I had to have a buzz to go out. I never went out sober, never. Why drink out when you can start at home. It made no sense to me that people would go out and drink two drinks. Who drank two drinks? I never could comprehend that.

I grinned and bore it and had dinner with my Mother at least once a week. We would have the basic dinner discussion about work and the family, and practically every night afterwards, I would go out to meet friends and drink. I came home whenever I pleased, if I even came home. In the morning I would be greeted by my happy mother. I hated the feeling I had every morning being completely hung over. I would tell my mom that I wasn't awake yet and needed some coffee. I was never nice or chipper to my mother. Only much later would I realize I was harboring subconscious resentments against her and my father from their divorce, which I didn't even know affected me.

My poor mother, if she only knew certain things I had done throughout my life, she'd be mortified. One evening after Vin and I had been partying, I was so wasted that I came up with the great idea of bringing him home with me. Sure, made perfect sense. Mom got up early and was out of the house by 7:00 A.M. She would never know. That was one of the most humiliating stunts I did in my last year of drinking -- the not caring about the outcome of any situation I put myself into as well as the constant lying and manipulation I would put my family and friends through to conceal it. My mom never asked me directly about my slumber guest, but mentioned it to my sister who, of course, covered for me.

Summer soon came, and Mom was barely home at all. She was a member of a shore house and spent all of her weekends in Avalon. Friday afternoon until Monday morning. It worked out wonderfully for me and Vin, and whomever else I wanted to bring home. Plus, I now had a house to party in since Vin's attic at his grandmother's house had become a less than desirable dwelling. That's being nice. It was filthy beyond belief.

My drugging and drinking escalated at this point, and I felt like shit all the time, was spending too much money on party favors, and was bitchier on a good day than when I was PMSing. Vin and I started fighting a lot, and he pissed me off so much one evening, that I told him to stop calling me. He did and we didn't speak for several weeks.

July 4th was coming up soon, and I really wanted to get away. An intelligent idea that came to me during a sober moment was to drive ten hours from Philadelphia to Indiana and visit Matty—someone who knew me and loved me unconditionally, someone I felt comfortable with. I weathered the arduous trip, but my ass hurt from driving so much. I think I had permanently dented my driver's seat from the cross-country drive the prior Fall. I made it there in one piece feeling like hell from drinking the night before. I wondered what would happen if I got pulled over in a hung-over state. Although there was no present alcohol in my system, surely there was some residual ether from the night before. I arrived in Indiana at 7:30 P.M. and was relieved and happy to see Matty. We did what we do best. We partied. Matty had some leftover Vicodin from a recent back surgery, and I gobbled them up like Sweet tarts. I took one when we were drinking at the local strip club; we liked to spice it up a bit. I felt a little woozy and almost nauseous, and after a few minutes, I got sick in the bathroom. Minutes later I felt fine and kept on drinking. The problem was the effect didn't last longer than an hour or so. So, I asked for another one and another one and another one. Matty cut me off after four. The next night I swiped six or seven pills from his stash before we even started drinking. I told Matty I took a couple, and he didn't seem to mind, until he counted his stash and realized just how many I did take. He was irate and wouldn't give me any more. Jeez, my own drug partner wouldn't even give me any more drugs.

After my drive home from the holiday weekend I was tired and told myself, yet again, that I would slow down my lifestyle and focus solely on my career. My job in Princeton was going quite well, though I showed up at work hung-over a few times a week. I continued to be a high-functioning alcoholic, always showcasing motivation and drive to my employer. I lived on double shots of espresso to propel my morning work routine, and by lunch time I would hit a wall and start ingesting power bars and diet Cokes.

I had befriended a female co-worker in my office, who knew of my extra curricular evenings, and she lived vicariously through me, eager to hear about my escapades. I would enter my office in the morning and call her into my office, asking if I smelled of booze or not. Holding her nose and waving her hand, she would give me Altoids to mask any hint of lingering alcohol on my breath. I started carrying a travel size of Scope with me in my purse.

September 2003
My Own Apartment
Wayne, Pennsylvania

By August I knew I had to find my own place since summer would soon be over, and Mother would stop going to the shore every weekend. I really wanted to get my own apartment and have my own things back. I was tired of living with my family. However, I wasn't sure I wanted to give up my California ties. If I moved into my own apartment, that would surely solidify my geographical options. I couldn't get back to California any time soon, and I'd have to fork over $2,000.00 to move my belongings out of storage and have it shipped cross-country. Did I really want to do this? I struggled with this decision for a few weeks and finally decided to stay in Valley Forge for the time being.

In early September, right before I moved into my apartment, I sought Vin out after not seeing him for weeks. It wasn't too hard to find him. He spent most nights at the local watering hole. I was bored with whichever man was in my rotation and decided I wanted some normalcy. The fact that I saw Vin as being normal was scary in its own right. We started seeing each other again, though by this time, I had already been getting Joey from our twenty-three-year-old Belize drug dealer who worked as a cook in a local restaurant. I was also sleeping with Belize Boy here and there, and although he rarely gave me free coke, I felt like a coke whore. The sex was crazy Latin lover sex, and after a few weeks, it was just too much to keep it going, so I ended it with Belize Boy. I could still get Joey from him whenever I needed to as he didn't want to lose one of his best customers. He was no dummy.

My firm's Newport Beach office hadn't seemed interested in having me join their team. But then again, I didn't ask. I should have— before I spent over $2,000 to move my stuff back to Philly. In mid-October, the President in the Newport Beach office heard that I was interested in possibly returning to California. He called and asked if I'd want to move back. I couldn't believe it. How could I possibly think about moving away again? And yet, I did.

By mid-December I made the decision. I'd spent only four months in my own apartment in Philly before geographic number fifteen, but who was counting?

My bon voyage happy hour was set for early February, and my move-out date was February 20th, 2004. I had one of my regular daters with me that night, and the next night I met up with Vin. I continued this trade-off until I left Pennsylvania. Insanity at its best.

I was nervous, excited and full of uncertainty about this move. I felt torn between doing the right thing for my career and leaving my family, yet again. My new company gave me a promotion, a raise and a fully paid relocation package back to San Diego. I went on an apartment hunting trip in mid-January and settled on a cute one bedroom apartment in the Village of Carlsbad. This was close enough to my scene in San Diego and only about a forty-five minute drive to my new office in Orange County. I lived four blocks from the center of town, which was the main criteria, since I wanted to be sure that I could walk home from the bars and clubs and not worry about driving. I already had one DUI, I didn't need another one.

My last week in Valley Forge consisted of non-stop happy hours and group dinners with anyone and everyone. Old friends, new friends, some long-forgotten friends and the

family get-togethers. I was leaving my
wreckage behind and off to another fresh start.

Chapter 16

February 2004
Merrywood Apartments
Carlsbad, California

The Boeing 747 hit the tarmac hard on my arrival flight into San Diego, and my heart raced as I was ready to get back to business and start living my life the way I did thirteen months before. Kinda like the way I already had been living it back East. During my first month, I focused on getting re-acclimated with my former home. I stared spending time with Kristen again, but she was trying to get sober.

What? Why?

That didn't make any sense to me. Her ex-boyfriend, Bryan, was over a year sober through Alcoholics Anonymous, an organization that I had no intention of researching. Kristen would come over and drink with me, and sometimes she wouldn't drink with me. Either way, I never asked her why she kept going to *those meetings*.

It felt strange to be back in San Diego, back to a place that seemed lonely without Matty, and I couldn't help but wish he still lived there. Being alone gave me a lot of time to think, and I was miserable. I was scared my life would be the same cycle of drugs and drinking that it was before. I wanted a fresh start and didn't want to get sucked back into the vortex of ferocious partying. I yearned to get my life together and ease up on the drinking, and especially the drugging. I was almost thirty-seven years old, and I was tired of the habits my life revolved around. I had nothing significant to show for it.

Almost immediately, I became extremely homesick and lonely, more alone than I had ever felt. I drank at home every night, normally alone, since Kristen and I weren't joined at the hip any longer. I quickly became more and more depressed and despondent. I couldn't tell anyone that, though, nor could I complain to anyone. Who would listen? Moving back to San Diego is what I wanted, or so I thought. But I soon realized this wasn't the case.

My thirty-seventh birthday was on Wednesday, March tenth. I don't remember exactly what I did to celebrate. I am sure I drank. On Saturday March twentieth, I received my second DUI, the one in front of the well-lit liquor store at midnight with Ernie and Lisa in tow.

Kristen's father is a lawyer and his firm provided my representation, especially concerned over the question of whether or not the State of California would find out about my first DUI in Pennsylvania. If so, and the states were reciprocal, I would have an eighteen-month license suspension with no leeway. However, if this was considered my first DUI in California, I would receive a six month suspension with the caveat that I could get a special driving permit to travel to and from work. At this point in time, I was hoping that the State of California would find out about the Pennsylvania arrest so I could run back to Philadelphia and not deal with this problem. I told myself there was no way I was going to have a suspended license for a year and a half out here, no fucking way. It just wouldn't work with my current commuting situation, and I knew that whatever life had in store for me would answer my burning question of where I would end up. I just had to wait it out until my court hearing in mid-June, three months away.

In addition to the two DUIs I did receive, I must confess that I had at least two sidestep situations where I should have received DUIs.

In San Diego one evening in 2001, I had left a house party in an area of town I wasn't very familiar with. I ended up going the wrong way down a one-way street. Idiotic by any standard. A female cop pulled me over and started asking the normal questions.

"Have you been drinking?"

The normal follow up question, "What have you had to drink tonight?"

And, flashlight shining on my face to reveal my dilated pupils, the worst question of all, "How much have you had?"

I knew I was fucked. Minutes later her dispatch radio signaled to her. She left me pickling in my own fear for a moment and then returned. "It's your lucky night, Miss. There was a shooting two blocks from here and I need to go. Please drive safely home." With that she scurried along.

Again, the foxhole prayer had worked that evening. But then reality set in. A shooting two blocks away had occurred. Where was I? The ghetto? I had to start hanging out more in La Jolla.

Another time I was pulled over when I was back East with expired California plates and registration on my car, so very responsible of me. This was during my year hiatus where I ran back home for solace and safety, which I didn't find. It was also the year before I quit drinking.

It was 11:30 P.M. on a Saturday night in Berwyn and I veered into the parking lot of a local bar I frequented. A cop pulled in right behind me and started questioning the legality of my vehicle. He was very nice and pleasant and showed no air of concern. He approached me as I was locking my car and asked why my car had California plates. Shaking like a washing machine on spin cycle, I explained to him that I was moving back to California in two weeks and hadn't been able to legally register it yet. He acquiesced, telling me I should at least get legal Pennsylvania registration until I left. I agreed with him, thanked him and he went on his merry way. Surprised that he never asked if I was drinking, I wondered if he could imagine how truly thankful I was that evening, especially since it was late, and I had already consumed numerous glasses of red wine. I remember walking into the bar and feeling victorious. I ordered a stiff drink and scored some coke. Whew, glad that was over with.

Three days after my Carlsbad DUI, I continued drinking at home every night. Two bottles of wine, (which later turned into box wine – it was so much easier!) A bottle of vodka, cheap bottles of champagne, whatever it took for me to escape. I ventured out with my friends, who were trying to cheer me up, but even that didn't satisfy me. I was so disgusted with myself, and felt I wasn't good enough to be seen with them or out in public at all. The self-loathing and self-hatred made me not want to leave my apartment. I didn't want anyone to see me.

In the last few years of my drinking, I imbibed every night just to numb out and fall asleep. Weekends were always the best, because I could justify drinking earlier in the day with Bloody Mary's or Mimosa's since no one was around to monitor or judge me. On Sunday nights, I would have episodes of paranoia after drinking through the forty-eight hour weekend.

The anxiety attacks would occur early in the evening around 6:00 P.M., and I would have to drink more wine just to make sure I could fall asleep later. The dread of going back to reality on Monday filled me with fear. I would rock myself to sleep and hope that I wouldn't wake up in the morning.

My only bright spot in the month of April was that Matty was coming to visit me for a long weekend. I couldn't wait. My old comfortable shoe arrived on a Thursday evening, and by Friday morning we hit the pavement. Since I couldn't drink and drive, I would drink one cocktail during our afternoon activities and then switch to Diet Coke to drive to our next stop. This was insufferable for me, but I forged ahead for his sake and continued on with the Del Mar bar crawl. Poseidon, Jimmy O's, Epazote, En Feugo and dinner at Bully's. Matty was fully aware of my second DUI, and him being in his own disease of addiction also, understood how scared I was about my impending future. But he too wanted what he wanted what he wanted. There was no stopping us. This was all we knew together.

After dinner, we had to meet Joey. Just like old times. We drove home where I could drink and drink and drink and stayed up until 6:00 A.M. Saturday morning and then slept most of the day. Our same routine continued until Tuesday when he left town. I felt even worse after Matty left. The feeling of abandonment and loneliness came back the minute I dropped him off at the Airport. My only solace was drinking my wine, smoking my cigarettes and watching reruns of Sex and the City. I blamed California and my company for the latest misfortunes in my life. I had almost begged Matty to let me move to Indiana so I could be with him. He didn't bite. Again, I felt rejected by someone I cared about.

Kristen had suggested to me that I should go to an Alcoholics Anonymous meeting. She commented that the court would make me go to AA meetings when I got convicted of my DUI anyway. It was late April and the last thing I wanted to do was go to an AA meeting. Kristen was now sober for a few weeks. I was stupefied that she didn't drink any more, at least not that I saw. I just couldn't imagine it. It's amazing that not once did I ever ask my sober friend Kristen about the program. I was in complete denial that I was a real alcoholic.

One night we did attempt to go to an Alcoholics Anonymous meeting in Carlsbad, but when we got there it was a men's meeting. Bummer. We went out for Mexican food, and I drank Coronas until I went home and started drinking from my wine stash.

In early May, I finally decided to go to a meeting with Kristen and see what this AA thing was all about. I had only heard about AA through movies and TV, specifically *NYPD Blue* and the Meg Ryan tear jerker, *When a Man Loves a Woman.* That was it. I loved drug and alcohol movies however: *Casino, Good Fellas, Traffic, Rush, 28 Days,* and *Leaving Las Vegas.* Anytime a new alcohol or drug movie came out, I couldn't wait to go see it. It was almost like I wanted to see where my addiction was in comparison to someone else's. I had to make sure I wasn't going off the deep-end and could rationalize that my drinking and using was justified because I wasn't as bad as those actors playing in a movie – although I knew to my inner core that I was as bad as they were. I just wasn't ready to see it yet.

Kristen and I planned to meet at the local Starbucks for an 8:00 P.M. meeting in Encinitas. However, she was running late that evening and called to say she'd just meet me at the meeting. GASP! I had to walk in there alone. *Alone?* Fuck, I was pissed. Jesus Christ.

I parked my car on the street across from the meeting and sat there for a couple minutes to psyche myself to get out of the car. Fuck, Fuck, Fuck is all I could say to myself.

Screw it, get out of the car and go to the meeting; you can do it. Go! Get out!

I opened the car door and started walking toward the insignificant address. The meeting was located on Second Street in Encinitas, off the Pacific Coast Highway. I opened the door and people turned, I felt everyone scrutinizing me when I entered. They did, I was a newcomer. At the time I had no idea what that meant. Anyone who has less than ninety days of sobriety is considered a newcomer. I took a seat in the back of the room in the nice plastic lawn chair that was so generously provided by the Fellowship. I started listening to what was being read.

How it Works, Chapter 5 from the Big Book of Alcoholics Anonymous. Within minutes I was stricken with the *Oh Shits*.

Oh Shit, I definitely have a problem, and I need to be here.

Oh Shit, am I going to have to stop drinking or can I have a drink once in a while?

Oh Shit, how will I live my life without alcohol? That isn't going to work. Are you sure I could be an alcoholic? I don't think so. I'm not drinking out of a brown paper bag, peddling for change. I'm not hiding my flask in my desk drawer, and I am not drinking in the morning when I get up. Did Bloody Mary's count? That's not drinking. That is the social cocktail that goes with breakfast.

I sat in that meeting with my head down the whole time and never looked around. I couldn't wait for it to be over so I could go home and drink. After the meeting, a couple of people approached me and told me to keep coming back. Again, clueless as to what that meant, I wondered why would I keep coming back if I didn't have to? I told Kristen I'd call her tomorrow and took off quicker than you can say *alcoholic*.

Driving home from the meeting, I started feeling like maybe I could stop drinking for a little bit. I could clear the cobwebs and rejuvenate my liver, get back on my feet. I went home and opened up a bottle of wine like any good alcoholic would. I didn't know about this whole AA thing. Maybe I didn't need to quit drinking all together.

The next day was May fifth. I flew back to Philadelphia to visit my family for the first time since I'd moved in February, but also because it was my god-daughter's first holy communion. It was the god-motherly thing to do. I went home and drank for five straight days. I saw my family, friends, and an occasional guy I had dated back home. I also had my moment of clarity.

I was with Suzy. She and Hank hosted a pre and post-dinner party with Jenny and her husband also. We drank a good amount of wine that evening, and ironically, I thought we didn't have enough. We had eight bottles for six people, and two of them were magnums. What was I going to drink when we finished all the wine? After dinner, we went back to Suzy's house to chill out and play pool. Me and my date were going to sleep in their guest house that night so we could keep the party going. I don't know exactly what the discussion was between myself and Suzy, but I got choked up and started tearing. I walked outside and lit a cigarette. Suzy followed.

My clarity came when I broke down in tears and told her that my life was shit. I remember telling her specifically, *everything bad that has ever happened to me in my life was because of my drinking and drugging*. I had an unmanageable and miserable life because of my addictions. I needed help.

She, of course, thinking this was just drunk talk, consoled me and tried to make me feel better. "Well, yeah maybe if you quit drinking for a while, you'd feel better. At least until your DUI situation is resolved. Don't worry Nance it will all work out....I love you."

On Monday, May tenth, I had dinner with my Dad at his house where I only drank one glass of wine. I knew I was going to be at an old friend's house after dinner and would be driving my Dad's car. My father didn't know that I'd just been served my second DUI a few weeks earlier.

In driving the thirty minutes to my friend's house, I stopped at the liquor store near his home in Wilmington, Delaware. I bought a magnum of red wine. I don't remember the brand, which didn't matter. I drank a few glasses of wine, and my friend only had two. He had a big meeting in the morning. What a wimp. We watched a couple of episodes of the Sopranos, and at 11:00 P.M., he went up to go to bed. I told him I'd be up in a minute. There was a fourth of a bottle of wine left. I couldn't leave it there. I had to drink it right then and there.

I picked up the bottle and started drinking it. I didn't even use the nice crystal-stemmed wine glass. Who needed glasses? They were just obstacles in getting the wine to my lips. I remember standing in the center of the dimly lit den. I realized the way I was polishing off the wine wasn't dignified or classy. I had drunk from a liquor bottle numerous times before. This time it felt different. It felt desperate. It felt rash.

It was my last drink.

I feel the whole purpose in my move back to California was to get me sober, and God had intervened. He wanted me to get help and served me that second DUI as my wake-up call. The alarm clock had gone off and, for once, I didn't hit my snooze button.

Chapter 17

May 2004
Alcoholics Anonymous Fellowship
Encinitas, California

The first few weeks of my sobriety weren't charming. I wasn't reaping any of the benefits that sobriety had to offer. PAWS, post-alcohol withdrawal syndrome, overwhelmed me as I didn't believe initially that I was that bad of a drunk. I just liked to drink every day. Did I really do that much damage?

My mind was in a daily fog, barely functioning at half-capacity. I had incredible insomnia, and when I did sleep, it was for hours and hours, and I cried on a daily basis, especially after I'd leave a meeting. PAWS also delivered extreme short-term memory loss. I would brush my teeth three times in the morning, not remembering if I had just brushed them or not. While at work, I would call a potential candidate to recruit, and minutes later I would call them again not recalling that I had just spoken with them. Besides the fogginess and my robotic state of mind, my attention span at work was limited, and I would have to leave early or come in late, using any excuse I could. I was dizzy and seeing spots and actually didn't think I was that bad. Ha-ha again.

The fact that I truly was an alcoholic hadn't set in yet, but the reality of my unmanageable life could not be denied. I knew I was in the right place. I soon realized I had no real control over my drinking; no matter how many times I had tried to stop on my own, I couldn't.

At day two of sobriety, Kristen had asked me if I wanted to attend a Speaker's meeting in Carlsbad. She explained to me that someone shares their story at the meeting, and it's not a discussion meeting. Not having any idea what that meant, I agreed to go. We walked into the Town Hall, where the mix was so eclectic; it looked like the Harley Convention was invited to a Tupperware party. Within ten minutes I saw someone I knew.

Oh shit, run. That was my first reaction.

She was a former colleague of mine named Karen. I remembered hearing that she was in AA and thinking, "Wow, good for her," all the while gloating to myself, I'm glad I'm not that bad. Hello, black kettle, this is pot calling!

I decided to be an adult and walked over to Karen, and said "Hi." She didn't seem at all surprised to see me and was welcoming. There is one thing I'll never forget that Karen said to me. She said she came to AA to stop drinking, but this program changed her life. *Changed her life.* How was that possible?

I dismissed what she said and thought she was in over her head and that the cult of AA had engulfed her. I surmised that all of the other women there were also freaks, since after introducing myself as a newcomer, I was tagged. At least six women approached me and gave me their phone numbers during the break. I had no idea why. They kept saying to me, "Keep coming back." Was something going to happen to me? Was I going to win a door prize? Was God himself going to welcome me during my next visit?

When I had achieved six full days of sobriety, Kristen mentioned a Monday Night Women's Meeting that I could attend. I wasn't sure what the Women's Meeting agenda was about, so I decided to explore it further. The meeting was held at the Seacoast Community Church where a God dynamic became present.

Growing up Catholic, I had always believed in God, but felt he had deserted me, and I'd fled the church in my late teens. I didn't understand what he wanted from me, and I wasn't willing to explore it, but I accepted it as part of my life. Instinctively I knew I wasn't living by the principles of the Catholic Church or any church for that matter, so why be part of it? I attended mass yearly at Christmas, Easter and the occasional wedding and funeral. Only when I had to. This presence was soon going to be thrust into my life, and I tentatively listened.

I walked into the Women's meeting where a group of thirty-five women were smiling, talking, drinking coffee and laughing. Ill at ease, I felt out of my comfort zone. I walked over to the first open seat I saw where I placed my Red Bull and purse and walked out of the room to escape into the bathroom. I walked into the ladies restroom and observed a woman drying her hands with a paper towel. Something about her seemed warm and inviting; she was attractive, appeared to be in her late thirties, and wore stylish clothes. I could have envisioned myself drinking with her at a ritzy bar ordering top shelf vodka martinis. She smiled and said *hi* to me. Instantly I felt a connection with her.

The Women's meeting began in the normal fashion, reading the AA Preamble, Chapter Five, How it Works and then honoring certain individuals with tokens. You received tokens for sobriety milestones of thirty, sixty, ninety days, six months, nine months and every year thereafter of sobriety.   A young girl named Mandy was taking a six-month token.

Mandy was in her early thirties, petite with long shiny dark hair. Her smile stretched from ear to ear. I couldn't imagine that this sweet cute girl was an alcoholic. I thought she was in the wrong place. After she took her token, she shared how the past six months changed her life and how this program had saved her. She shared some of her drinking story, and I was in awe. She talked about how many cars she had wrecked, how many nights she drank herself into a blackout, and how she used to hide forty-ounce beers in her purse and would drink them on the train ride home from work. This little girl did that? Wow. I guess I really was one too, because I knew I was as bad, if not worse, than Mandy.

In the first couple of weeks of my sobriety, I kept having women reach out to me and giving me their phone numbers. Why would I call them? If I wanted to drink, call them? I wanted the men to give me their phone numbers, not the women. I found it very peculiar and they also kept asking me if I had a sponsor. I felt like an outsider because I didn't have one, but I also wasn't sure I wanted one since it would mean I'd have to stick around for a while. I decided to call a woman I'd met at the Women's meeting. Her name was Sharon, and I remember the night I called her, I was nervous and apprehensive.

When I had to call someone I didn't want to, i.e. a guy, I would have a drink. I couldn't do that in this situation, so I sat and struggled with whether or not I should call her. Finally, I thought, get over yourself and do it. I reached into my kitchen drawer of phone numbers, found hers, and picked up the phone. I was more scared to ask Sharon to be my sponsor than to admit that I was an alcoholic. She answered on the third ring. Damn it, I'd sorta hoped I'd get her voicemail. Butterflies were fluttering in my stomach.

"Hi, is this Sharon?"

She replied, "Hey, how ya doing?"

Did she know it was me? "Hi, it's Nancy from the Monday night women's meeting."

She replied, "I know, I'm glad you called."

The rest of our conversation was easy, and I was surprised she knew who I was. I soon asked if she would be my sponsor, and she accepted. She was the first angel that was put in my life. She was that stylish woman in the bathroom.

My colleagues in Newport Beach didn't know about my alcoholism. I had confided to two women in our Princeton office who were also friends outside of work, so it felt safe to tell them. I eventually had to tell my assistant in Newport Beach because my weekly tardiness and early departures were now a habit and I felt I needed to let someone know what was going on. She was very understanding and explained to me that her sister-in-law had over ten years of sobriety in AA. I felt better just knowing that.

My biggest relief in early sobriety was that I was relieved. The monkey was off my back. I didn't feel the need to drink anymore. What a freedom this was for me. I didn't have to lie, manipulate, cheat or control my life any longer. I could let life unfold without trying to maneuver it to make it work for me. I knew I could be a control freak at times, but in getting sober you realize just how much you do try and control the elements in your life. Sobriety also made me feel that life would work out the way it was supposed to.

If I knew then, what I now know about AA, I'm not sure I would have been so willing to get sober. If someone said to me "You can never drink again," I wouldn't have signed on the dotted line. I'd originally figured I could do some marijuana maintenance, but I couldn't find any, since that was never my drug of choice. I bought a bottle of whipped cream and decided to do whippets from a Reddi-Whip canister, but I soon learned that would be considered a relapse. Anytime you take any substance to *change the way you feel* – that's considered a relapse. I guess some folks say nicotine and caffeine could be considered a relapse, but no - that's not really the way it works – at least for me. I'm sure there are a lot of different opinions out there in the world of recovery and hypocrisy. Let's just say I soon became addicted to Starbucks and energy drinks. Red Bull without Absolut, what a switch.

In addition to the women's meetings, I was regularly attending meetings at the mixed fellowship on Second Street in Encinitas. This became my home away from home and the place I felt safest. This was my Betty Ford Clinic, except there were no Hollywood stars— or none that I knew of; it was an anonymous program. The thought of going into a treatment center before I got sober never occurred to me. I believed that no one went to a rehab center, unless they were heroin addicts or famous. I imagined going to Promises in Malibu where Ben Affleck and the Osbourne kids got sober. However, I don't think I would have been going into that facility with best intentions. I had just wanted to see the stars, not face problems and become responsible for my life.

When the idea of getting help did occur to me, I realized that I would rather eat dirt than tell my family or co-workers about my problem. I decided to do this gig on my own. Getting sober without the initial support of my family and friends back East led me to reach out to AA which responded in a manner that made me feel comfortable. They told me early on that they would love me until I could learn to love myself. It took months for that to sink

in. Clearly, I had found a miracle on Second
Street.

In my first three weeks of sobriety, I was
fortunate enough to befriend several
courageous alcoholic women in the program.
They became my best friends and my AA
family. They listened to me, they understood
me, they let me cry, and they knew me. There
is nothing like connecting with another
Alcoholic. Nothing at all. We're a group of
people that all have the same thing in common,
and we can relate to what each other is feeling.
Every Alcoholic has a need to be accepted and
feel a part of a group. We've all felt it in our
lives and know that feeling of despair and
utter defeat. Desperation is a huge motivator.

These three close friends were Diana,
Tanya and Kella, all three blonde–haired, blue-
eyed beauties with a couple of months ahead
of me in their recovery, and each one radiated
happiness.

Tanya and her husband were coke and
booze partiers, like me. They owned a
flourishing sports agency, managing Motor-
cross racers, which kept her husband running
around the race circuit, representing his clients
and indulging in the lifestyle that young
athletes enjoyed. Tanya was home as the

mother of three children, and at 4:00 P.M. every day she would start drinking her wine. This was her reward for managing her domestic life of child-rearing and keeping house. She deserved this wine.

That is how most alcoholics felt when they drank; it was justified. I just got a promotion; Drink! I just got a new car; Drink! I had a fucked-up day; Drink! I cheated on my husband….with his best friend, Drink! Whatever the excuse was, good or bad; we drank, no matter what. It fueled our denial and rationalizing. We needed that drink. We had to have that drink.

Before having children, Tanya was a party gal and enjoyed a carefree lifestyle scurrying around with her husband. As soon as she started having children, she knew she had to slow down, but her husband didn't. Soon they were fighting frequently about his absences from home and his drinking on the road and at home. She came to Alcoholics Anonymous through Al-Anon. Al-Anon is the sister program of Alcoholics Anonymous where you attend meetings to help you manage the Alcoholic in your life. Tanya attended an Al-Anon meeting while pointing the finger at her husband for his drinking and drugging, all the while in denial about her own drinking problem. She realized that she couldn't stop drinking her wine nor drugging with her husband when he would come home in between Motor-cross tours.

She told him she wanted to get sober, but he dismissed her advice and continued his life with the motorboys. Wanting a different life for her and her children, Tanya decided she would go to AA meetings at Second Street, got a sponsor and started working the twelve-step program. She soon visited an attorney and had divorce papers drawn up. She wanted out of her marriage if her husband wouldn't change his warrior ways. Today Tanya is a sober mother to her kids and still a close friend.

Blonde beauty number two is Diana, she spent the past ten years in San Francisco, where she managed a million dollar bond fund for a nationally known investment house. She was successful, owned a home in the Bay Area, spent time there with her well-to-do boyfriend, and lived a charmed existence–drunk the majority of the time. She was accomplished and seemed to have the world in her hand. However, she was miserable.

Yet, like me—and most alcoholics, she didn't want to quit drinking. She knew she was an alcoholic from her college days but couldn't bring herself to admit it. Diana had a brother who was six years sober, though five years younger, and an Aunt who had also turned to sobriety, so Diana was well aware of Alcoholics Anonymous. She wanted to escape her life, though, and one day walked into work and quit. Diana put all of her belongings in storage and left to travel abroad for a year. She spent the summer in Nantucket with a boyfriend who wanted to marry her—too much reality; she fled to Europe. In Europe she visited countries where she couldn't drink, so, at a duty free airport, she purchased a bottle of vodka and drank it in the ladies room. Hours later on a plane, she awoke in Bangkok with just her passport and no personal effects. She knew she needed help.

She arrived back in the States to visit her family for Christmas and stayed with her parents. On Diana's first days at home, she drank wine and hid it from her parents. She decided to detox herself while attending a Yoga retreat in Mexico. That didn't help any and she found herself drinking and meditating to Ghandi. Made perfect sense to me. Diana got worse. She came back to San Diego, called her brother and told him she needed help. He took her to a meeting.

Diana started attending meetings regularly in late December but didn't get sober until February and would show up at meetings drunk and would drink in between meetings. She couldn't stop. Then on February 3, 2004 she woke up and didn't have another drink; she surrendered. Diana can't say exactly what made her stop, but she does know that something inside her and above her was instrumental on that special day. Diana is still sober today and lives with her boyfriend in Santa Barbara and practices Yoga on a daily basis.

Diana was thirty-six and Tanya was thirty-four when I met them. Seeing both of them as accomplished and attractive women who had the guts to get help gave me hope that if they could survive the last couple of months, maybe I could too.

The second week of being sober, I met my sober bestie, Kella. Kella, whose real name is Kelley, had changed her name when she got sober. Thanks to a barista at Starbucks who jotted her name incorrectly on a coffee cup, she became Kella. She was twenty-nine years old, married and the mother of three young children. She is a bombshell, a real southern California girl. Kella dressed in hip surfer attire; her signature style, along with a petite body, long golden hair and a gorgeous smile. She caused all the men to take a double glance towards her when she enters a room. Kella scared me at first because she seemed a bit nuts. She had a militant sponsor who knew the program inside and out and, who I thought, had brainwashed Kella a bit, but I knew nothing at that point and assumed Kella needed a lot of help. Truth is we are all sick people with an incurable disease who need help. Kella's lunacy was something I related to since I also felt wacky. We were both standing on the edge and teetering just to hold on. Before long we were talking daily and laughing. That's what I remember in the early days, the laughter. Sheer pure and crazy laughter. It sure made me keep wanting to come back.

Kella had tried to get sober numerous times before and lasted barely thirty days each time. She had spent time in treatment centers, detox centers and even psychiatric facilities. Her favorite movie is, *Girl Interrupted.*

Say no more. I get it.

Kella married her high school boyfriend at age nineteen and started having babies soon thereafter. She lived in a beautiful four-bedroom home and played the part as perfect mom and housewife. However, she drank all day long. Driving her kids to school, she would have a six-pack in the center console of her car and not think twice about it. She would disguise her beer in a coffee tumbler and no one suspected it. Real alcoholics have a way of not *acting* that drunk; they can control it, when need be. The shame and remorse she felt in putting her children in harm's way was immense and she hated herself and desperately wanted to stop. She finally entered another treatment facility and had quit drinking three months before I got sober. This was the longest period she had gone without a drink since she was a teenager.

Forty days into my sobriety, I started experiencing feelings that I hadn't felt before, or if I did, I would have gotten drunk because of them. I would call and complain to Kella, who knew precisely what I was going through as she'd just experienced it a few weeks prior. It was eerie, but also reassuring to know that other people, woman like me, were experiencing similar episodes of anxiety, hypersensitivity and sadness. These were some of the same feelings I had experienced before I got sober, however, they came out in different pores of my body and evaporated into the air without a trace of recent alcohol. It felt like my body was trying to spit out any remnants of alcohol that was impacted into my bones; I was still in detox mode.

While attending mixed meetings at Second Street with Kella, we came to realize there was an issue regarding the men in recovery. Most of them were pleasant enough and truly cared about your recovery, but there was another gang called the thirteen steppers. These are men that would prey on a newcomer who was vulnerable and try to sleep with them. God is watching you boys, behave.

But you soon remember that men are men. I was mortified when I heard this and kept my distance from any man that I thought was paying too much attention to me. The men were mainly older and not anyone that I would give a second glance to. Don't misunderstand, they were extremely nice, supportive and helpful, but I didn't want to give any of them the wrong idea. I wanted to befriend a man who I could relate to on a personal basis. Be careful what you wish for.

Chapter 18

Summer 2004
2nd Street
Encinitas, California

Sixty days into my sobriety, I was on my pink cloud. I couldn't believe I had quit drinking, and the best part was I had a whole new group of friends that also didn't drink. I was mystified with my new life and that I was still sober. I wanted to scream it from the La Jolla bluffs: I'M SOBER! After my ninety day milestone, I felt my head pop. It was finally clear. I'd often heard at meetings that it takes a full ninety days to physically detox your body from alcohol. I didn't believe it until my ninety-first day. I was sleeping better and was more aware of what was taking place around me. I found myself looking forward to going to a meeting every day, sometimes two.

Adding to my excitement in sobriety was that I had made another new friend, and it wasn't a gal pal. Kella and I were sitting at an 8:00 P.M., Second Street meeting on a Saturday night, which by itself is abnormal. Only two months earlier, attending an AA meeting on a Saturday night was the last place I'd ever have expected to be. Five minutes into the meeting, a thirty-something gentleman stormed into the meeting.

He looked confused as he made a beeline for the strong urn of coffee. He was fiddling with the Styrofoam coffee cup while pushing his messy brown hair back into his ball cap with certain irritation. As he surveyed the room, I surveyed him and recognized that he was green and new to the AA environment. This newcomer was handsome and looked somewhat put together – more than most that is. He was wearing clothes that could have appeared in a J. Crew catalogue. Swiftly he took a seat. His name was Ben, and he had just left, on his own accord, the La Jolla twenty-eight-day treatment center where high bottom drunks get sober. Ben escaped on his thirteenth day of treatment, and walked into an AA meeting. He later informed Kella and me that he didn't like the forceful style his counselor imposed upon him, so he packed his bag and walked out.

Ben commented that people from AA visited his treatment center daily and stressed the importance of keeping a program intact after leaving the center. Ben decided that he didn't need to spend any more money on treatment and would start going to AA meetings to get sober—and that is just what he did. He got out Saturday afternoon and came to a meeting Saturday night.

As an observer of others who have been in treatment, I've witnessed a high percentage of addicts who dive hastily back into their vices as soon as they are released. Whether its alcohol, drugs, food or gambling, real addicts think they just need a brief reprieve to start feeling regular again. Clearly that isn't the case. Just because you are clean and sober for twenty-eight days doesn't mean that life returns to normal. Staying clean and sober is a process and a lifestyle, and, shit, it's fucking hard to keep doing it on a daily basis. That's the main reason I go to a lot of meetings, because I forget. I forget what is was like, and I forget the message. My brain doesn't sustain information as it once did, and I need to recall certain phrases: *One day at a time, Keep it Simple, Keep coming back, Work with a sponsor, Do the Steps*. I need to hear all of those things and then some.

I need to hear the alcoholic mother with eleven days of sobriety share about her third DUI which spurred her husband to kick her out and not give her any privileges to see her kids. I need to hear the twenty-nine-year-old woman share that two months after getting out of treatment, she thought she could drink like a normal drinker, but instead, went out for *one drink* on a Thursday night and woke up Tuesday morning after a six-day coke binge and subsequently lost her job, emptied her checking account, and lost any sense of self-respect or dignity. Or worse yet, the bottom feeder drunk who has been living on the streets since his family disowned him ten years ago, and how he has been trying to get sober ever since, but who can't string together more than thirty days of sobriety.

I'm no different than any of those people; my story is different, but we're all the same. A bunch of drunks. Those stories keep me fresh and keep me in gratitude. I don't want to go back to the way I was living my life before, thanks, but no thanks. Alcoholics need as much help as possible and the hand of AA is always there; you just need to reach for it.

Ben and I struck-up a platonic friendship, and our friendship turned into an almost daily occurrence, talking on the phone, meeting at meetings, going to dinner after the meeting, and then during the weekend we would spend time together. We'd go to the beach, hit a Dave Matthews concert, or play tennis on a Sunday afternoon. Having a friend who was a man and someone that I could relate to without being wasted was such a welcome experience.

Ben was a cerebral overachiever and entrepreneur who at thirty-three had started his third technology company. He excelled academically at UCSD where he was financed by a Venture Capital firm in his senior year to start a technology company. One particular trait of many alcoholics is that they are high-functioning in some aspect of their lives, typically their careers. It is one of the delusions that we fool ourselves with: *if we still have our jobs, we're okay, we're not that bad*. But deep down we feel like a fraud and hope no one finds out. Ben knew he was an alcoholic for years, especially when his doctor informed him that he had more of his liver floating through his blood stream than what is normally considered healthy. Ben heard that tidbit of information four years before he quit drinking. What brought Ben to his surrender point happened on a morning while lumbering out of bed for his usual 9:00 A.M. wake-up call to get ready for work.

A girl was in his bed, a regular occurrence for him, and as he grunted to himself and shut the bedroom door, he wondered what the hell had happened last night. Grabbing a can of beer and entering the shower, the idea of being able to leave the beer on the bathroom vanity wasn't an option, as Ben needed it with him at all times. He turned the water spout on as hot as possible, entered the shower and then started washing his hair. Seconds later some shampoo splashed into his can of beer. Aghast, he went off the deep end, cursing himself and yelling while banging his fists against the shower wall – he had a breakdown. Soon thereafter he called Scripps Hospital. It was time to check in and get help.

I thought Ben was one of the smartest guys I had ever met, and of course, being tall, dark and handsome didn't hurt. We both shared the same witty and sarcastic jesting and genuinely liked to spend time together. We disclosed our crazy life stories to one another with candor and amusement.

Ben didn't jump into the program like most and didn't work a valid program with his sponsor. He would talk to me about his feelings and what was going on in his life. Unintentionally I became his sponsor, although it was never established. I learned that his brother was a pill addict who recently got clean and sober. I learned that his parents divorced when he was young leaving emotional scars he didn't even recognize, and I learned that he had been burned by numerous women in his past and would never trust another again. I also learned that Ben was a loner and didn't have any genuine friends. I started looking forward to seeing and talking to him on a daily basis and it felt like we were dating, without the romance and intimacy, and I found myself having feelings for him.

I decided to sit on them and wait a few weeks to see if he too maybe felt the same way. Weeks went by and I'd complain to Kella, "Ugh, I can't stand this anguish of not telling him how I feel, but I could never tell him how I feel, unless I was drunk, of course."

She would laugh and say, "Just tell him."

Sure, if only it could have been that simple.

I relayed my angst to my sponsor, and she commented, "He's not emotionally available for you; he has a lot of his own issues, and you're both newly sober. I don't recommend telling him how you feel."

Ideally, the AA fellowship suggests not getting involved in any emotional entanglements for your first year of sobriety. Screw that. I was thirty-seven years old, and no one was going to tell me if I could date or not. What are we, fifteen? I didn't want to believe what Sharon told me and was daydreaming for my fantasy chick flick to jump off the screen and become my reality again. I wanted to be *Sally* and him my *Harry*. Not being able to withstand my real feelings for him, I said *what the hell* and took a risk.

Originally, I sent him an email explaining how much I felt for him and how important he was to me. He backed off. I didn't hear from him for a week after sending the email and decided to phone him.

Sweaty palms and lighting a cigarette, I dialed.

"Hey there, how ya doing?" I said to him as I was driving to a meeting, hoping that he too was on his way to the same meeting.

"Heyyyyyyyyyy, what's up? I'm glad you called." Ben said.

He's glad I called? This is good.

"Yeah, why's that?" I waited in anticipation.

"I've been wanting to call you, and have just been busy. But, thank you very much for your email; it meant a lot to me. Ya know, I don't have a very good self-image of myself, and I appreciate all the nice things you said about me…."

But…I was waiting for the *but*; I could hear it in his voice.

He continued, "But, I've never had a women friend before, and your friendship means a lot to me, and I don't want to fuck that up."

I hesitated and thought, a man that I can't lasso in? Defeated, but head held high. "Of course, I completely understand, and thank you for your honesty. That means a lot to me. I'm glad too that we're friends; it's very cool."

Basically he said the typical bullshit a guy says when *he's just not that into you*. I didn't see him at that meeting that evening or hardly at any meetings anymore. He backed off for a couple weeks, but soon came back to the Fellowship, and we picked up where we left off and started talking and seeing each other again on a frequent basis.

Months went by and soon we entered year 2005. I was eight months sober, he was seven. Neither one of us had dated anyone yet, and we were still in our platonic friend mode, but as much as I did try to suppress them, my feelings only got stronger.

Knowing that I truly was living in a cinematic drama, I wanted to approach him again. I kept thinking, *maybe he's changed his mind, maybe's it's different now*. Doing the same thing over and over, and expecting different results--insanity at its best. Ben was alcohol to me, I couldn't put him down. A woman in the program suggested I tell him in person, face-to-face.

I laughed in her face, "Sure talk to him in person and tell him that? Sober?"

I waved her off and then realized that she was right. I needed to speak to him in person, and hear it from his own mouth, his own words. Working with Kella on what to say, I scribbled and scribbled and came up with a four sentence pitch on a post-it note.

I wanted to talk with you about something that's pretty important. I know you know how I've felt about you in the past, and as much as I have tried to suppress my feelings for you, I can't. You are the one person I want to talk to at the end of the day, and you get me, you get my career, my angst, and my issues – that means a lot to me and although we do have a great friendship, I want more.

I chose to say this to him the next time I saw him, which, of course, was going to be that night. We were going to see a band play at a saloon down the street from him. Ben played in a band and was always looking to see what his local competition was, thus we would frequent bars to evaluate other bands in the area. I would never have gone alone into this kind of venue, but with Ben I felt safe. We left the saloon around midnight and walking home on the sidewalk towards his house, I felt a pit in my stomach. A large wide open pit that was churning with my dinner from hours ago. My heart was beating more than if I had just done a snort of cocaine.

This was fucking grueling. *Duck my head in the toilet now, let's get it over with.* How was I going to say to him, soberly, what I was feeling? He was going to reject me, I knew that, but I still had to say it. I needed to speak my truth – for me, not for him. This was for me.

I pitched away, a curveball I might add, and he took it with stride. Thank goodness the street was dim, so I didn't have to look him in

271

the eye and could speak with my head down as we walked.

He answered in his kindest, most forthright way. "I'm flattered, I'm very flattered. But if I felt that way about you, you would have known by now. I'm sorry, I just don't feel that way for you, but I am very flattered."

Rejected again. Swallow it hard, Nance, and hold back the tears.

"Okay, well I had to ask, because I had to hear it from you. I needed to hear it directly from you in person. I'll be okay; not right now, but I will eventually."

Moments later, I walked away and said goodbye to him as I approached my car. He walked away, hesitated, and turned around towards me, smiling as he spoke "Hey, do you feel better yet?" His sarcastic wit wasn't wasted on me that evening.

"Nope, not yet, give me a week." I drove away and called Kella as tears streamed down my face.

I was crushed and felt like I was cast aside and dumped, even though we were never a couple. I cried for days and had to divert my meetings so I wouldn't see him. Slowly, ever so gingerly, Ben and I were able to become friends again. Looking back I am grateful I didn't date during my first year. I'm grateful I focused on my recovery and was able to know who I was – without anyone by my side to influence that. Ben was a diversion at a time when I probably needed one, but if it got any more entangled it would have erupted in my face and I emotionally wasn't able to manage being sober hardly, let alone being a relationship. *God was doing for me what I couldn't do for myself.*

Chapter 19

October 2004
Doctors, Diagnosis and Therapy
Encinitas, California

Entering fall, I felt spent physically and decided to make an appointment with my internist for a complete check-up and physical. I wanted to make sure all my counts were normal; cholesterol, thyroid, blood platelets, but most importantly that my liver was intact, and I was HIV free. Besides being borderline anemic, my liver was functioning normally, and my HIV screen was clean. However, after the physical detoxification from alcohol and drugs, I still had my mind to contend with. My true alcoholic thinking was rampant. I had to work on changing my behaviors and thought patterns, while also managing my emotions. Emotional sobriety is the most difficult part of sobriety for me.

I was starting to feel my feelings, real feelings, for the first time in my life. Before sobriety, when I was pissed off, I drank. When I was feeling blue, I drank. When I was in high spirits, I drank. When I was exhausted, I drank. When I felt ill, I drank. When I was uncomfortable, I drank. When I was in love, I drank. When I hated myself, I drank. When I was scared, I drank. When I was alone, I drank. When I was social, I drank.

I drank to erase every emotion I could. Screw them all. Who needed sensations and feelings, when you can just wash them away with alcohol? I didn't process my emotional feelings on any level. I never got to a point where I could because I would just start drinking again. Drinking for me was the cure all. I had to relearn life – how to exist in this world and how to feel *and* still be sober.

My emotional roller coaster was a loop-de-loop; some days I felt elated and other days I would fall into a dark hole where depression would fester. It would last a day or two, and I would isolate. I would go to meetings and work and that was it. I'd be in a state of self-pity and self hatred. Sleeping was a chore, because I couldn't sleep. I'd be up all night thinking about my past life, thinking about my future life, and not wanting to be in the present moment.

Manic in the middle of the night, I'd smoke, eat, and watch TV, anything to get out of my head. I felt I was going insane, yet again. For the most part, I was restless, irritable and discontent. I had to accept the fact that besides being powerless over alcohol and drugs, I was powerless over people, places and things. I couldn't manipulate others to get what I wanted and was told to just live in the moment. I was just along for the ride, and my safety bar wasn't fully locked.

Five months into my sobriety I found my fluffy pink cloud soon morphed into an ominous shade of grey. I was having trouble living my life sober. Life was a struggle, and I felt my sanity was at risk. I didn't want to drink or use, I just wanted to feel better. I never felt like this when I was drinking or using. If I did, I would self-medicate. I didn't want to be around. I wanted to join God in heaven and just check out. I didn't want to feel the pain anymore, and getting out of bed in the morning was becoming a challenge. I didn't want to think about my life--past, present or future. Experiencing any form of joy or serenity had disappeared, and life was a struggle. Why stick around for the misery?

I was never suicidal before I got sober. Sure, I thought about it like most people have – at one time – but this was distinctive. This was a conscious thought that occurred repeatedly, and I was scared. I felt like I would drink, but I didn't want to. Any sense of cognitive thinking I felt was lost. But I couldn't tell anyone how fucked up I felt, for fear they would think I was extreme, and not just an alcoholic. I didn't want to end up in the looney bin. I just wanted to go to sleep and not wake up. Taking a drink of poison, like Sleeping Beauty, sounded like a good alternative. I could wait for my prince to finally arrive.

One night after leaving a meeting I was chatting with other members of the fellowship and felt sane, as I normally felt when a meeting was over. Kella and I were talking. She knew what I was going through, as she too went through the psycho phase, as she called it, and commented that I should look into seeing a therapist. I waved her off and said that was too intense for me and that I was okay. I had already been in therapy–fifteen years ago–and had lied about my lifestyle, although now sober it might be different.

Naw, I didn't want to find out what else was wrong with me. Admitting and accepting that I was an alcoholic had been difficult enough. My thoughts of seeking outside help terrified me. Driving home from the meeting on the 5 north to go home, I got hysterical. I heard a song from my past that took me back to a dark period and unrestrained crying and madness overwhelmed me, and my driving became hazardous. I pulled over onto the shoulder and called Kella.

Crying and shaking, I spewed to her, "I don't know what's wrong with me. I don't want to do this anymore, but I don't want to drink. I can't stand this feeling–this feeling of nothingness. I hate the way I'm feeling. I don't want to be here. I want to check out. "

Kella completely understood, calmed me down and talked to me. She made me feel okay, and that what I was experiencing was normal for someone newly sober. I believed her, got back on the freeway, raced home and rocked myself to sleep.

I started seeing Kella's therapist, and within two visits she had diagnosed me as having *ultra rapid cycling bi-polar disorder*. Oh special. I wanted to send out the announcements quickly to family and friends so everyone could understand why I was such a moody bitch all the time. My therapist mentioned the fact that even though I was having bi-polar episodes today, in nine months or a year from now this may not be the case, and my brain and body might react differently then.

I had developed a chemical imbalance from all my years of cocaine and alcohol abuse. At first, this was very difficult for me to swallow, let alone believe. However, after having done my internet research on the disorder and how you get it, how to treat it and the particulars, I began to feel a tad better. Turns out that one of the key indicators is abuse of cocaine and alcohol. How fitting. Whether or not I had this disorder before age eighteen, I don't know. All I know is it made me feel better knowing this minuscule piece of information. In my non-sober years of not having to really feel my true feelings, it was nice to know that at least my attempts at trying to feel normal were in the right place. I felt vindicated in my abuse of alcohol and cocaine. It made sense to me that when I did abuse this fatal combination in abundance is when I felt okay.

This may sound a little skewed, I know. I mean, don't get me wrong, I abused these substances, but it was when I felt the most comfortable in my own skin. It's the feeling I always craved. However, I did quickly realize that this diagnosis did not make me a non-alcoholic. At first I thought maybe I'm not an alcoholic, and that's why I medicated with booze and coke. Delusion. I was in delusion and denial. A double-whammy. Denial is our demise. Alcoholics are always testing whether or not they are alcoholics. That is why some alcoholics relapse. They stop getting scared of being an alcoholic and start feeling comfortable living normal lives again and say to themselves, "Maybe I could go out and have a glass of wine."

After the wondrous diagnosis my psychiatrist gave me, I began really questioning whether or not *I really was an alcoholic*. If you're a normal social drinker, you're not concerned with what you did the night before because you were in control of your drinking and emotions. As alcoholics we lose all sense of morals, couth and, in my case dignity. I had a hard time realizing that I was a true alcoholic when I started in recovery. I kept asking myself, am I really that fucked? Can I never drink again? Should I be sitting in this AA meeting? Admitting I was an alcoholic wasn't anywhere near as difficult as accepting the fact. I finally was able to accept my disease and I was grateful that I finally had found out exactly what my ailment was. After years of searching for something, anything that would make me feel complete, I found it in giving up the drink. I'd known something was wrong with me for years, but I thought I was just fucked-up. Possessing crazy thinking is the cornerstone for being an alcoholic. The true definition of insanity is doing the same thing over and over expecting different results. Senselessly, I would say to myself in the evenings, *I'll just go out for one drink*. One drink was never in the cards for me, no matter how many times I would say to myself, *just one drink.* This mindset continually positioned me to consume many drinks throughout the night to the point where I would end up at the dive bar with the bottom feeder drunks I'd come to feel at home with.

Further driving me to accept my alcoholism was a score I received on my MAST test; Michigan Alcohol Screening Test. This was a test that was administered by the State of California if you were convicted of a DUI. I took this test when I attended my DUI class, another requirement by the State to fulfill my civic duty. It has questions like: Have you ever awakened the morning after drinking and found that you could not remember a part of the evening? Did you ever feel guilty about your drinking? Did you like to hide your drinking from others? I answered the test truthfully since I was sober when I entered the DUI program in June. A normal test score was less than seven points, I scored a whopping thirty-two points. Whew, finally a test that I had a high score on!

I also recognized that normal drinkers don't wonder if they're real alcoholics. They don't question their drinking on a daily basis, and they don't think about their drinking problem; they don't have one.

When I was in my first thirty days of recovery, I started working the twelve step program with Sharon. I thought reading the steps on the wall at the meeting was working the steps. I didn't think there was actual *work* involved. I look back now and laugh at how naïve I was in my early weeks of my recovery.

In the very first step, we admitted we were powerless over alcohol, that our lives had become unmanageable. Pen to paper, I had to write down my drinking life, specifically my life story as it pertained to my drinking and using, and for me this was writing from age thirteen to present day. Thirty pages later, I understood just how sick and powerless I was over alcohol and drugs.

I fully understood now what the step meant and for me I turned it around to grasp fully how fucked up my life truly was. *My life had become unmanageable, because I was powerless over alcohol.* In the next step, we were supposed to *"come to believe that a power greater than ourselves could restore us to sanity."* I had to find a higher power of my understanding. That was foreign to me since I was mad at God for so many years because he had screwed up my life by not answering my prayers when I needed him the most. Specifically, my love relationships with men. Up until I joined AA, I thought a man would fix me. Every time I started dating someone new, I would say to myself, "Okay, he is going to make my life complete and meaningful." Eventually I knew that this would never happen, and I filled that void even further with drugs and alcohol. They never failed me. I also recognized that I always picked men that drank and used as much as I did or more. Seldom did I date someone who didn't party like I did. That was an important trait for them to have. I remember saying to Suzy in my last year of drinking, "Well if he doesn't drink, there is no way I can date him."

HA! Sober guy, from a year prior, made it evidently clear that I couldn't sustain anyone who didn't drink. I ended up sabotaging our relationship when he told me I had a drinking problem. "Fuck you," was my answer to him.

My God turned out to be a higher power that I could understand and pray to. He wasn't the hypocritical Catholic God that I grew up with. Forty-five days into my sobriety, I had a spiritual experience which convinced me that my God showed up and was ready to get to work.

Sleeping one evening, as well as I could then, I had a dream, the kind of dream where you feel like you're really living it, and you're not dreaming. I was elevated on a large feathery platform bed nestled on a white cloud in the sky. I was sitting up in bed and leaning on my left side. Above me a light shone through, and an older man, who morphed into a vision of Santa Claus, Moses and Winston Churchill, flashed through the light and touched me. I jolted up from my dream and felt a presence in my room, a ghostlike and spiritual presence. I felt I had been touched by a spirit. It took me no time after that to *really* believe. I also felt that Maggie had entered back into my life in a spiritual way to help save me. She was my guardian angel to offer me salvation and I'd have to say, she's doing a pretty darn good job.

After the dream experience, I had to believe in Step 3. *Made a decision to turn our will and our lives over to the care of God <u>as we understood him.</u>* This was and still is a difficult step to live in. You do not control your life. Something greater than we are does, whether you call it God, the Ocean or your favorite pair of Manolo Blahnik's, something is out there controlling our lives and the outcome. Just let it be. I was relieved to get to this step so I could finally put the hammer down. The hammer that I kept hitting myself with over and over and over. I could stop playing God.

I worked through the steps, trusting in a higher power, trying to live by the golden rule and being of service to others, but then came step nine. Scary and humbling. Step nine requires you to make amends to everyone you may have hurt or screwed over in your former non-sober life. I had considerable wreckage to clean up and was hoping I could hire someone to do this for me. Shit, this one sucked. Couldn't we go back to Step Two when I had my God dream? At least I was sleeping for that one.

Sharon suggested that I start with the easier amends first. So, I started with Jenny, as she loved me unconditionally and never judged me. During one of my visits back home in my first year of sobriety, we had a day of sisterly activities planned – coffee, shopping at the mall, spa treatments and then ending the afternoon with a late lunch. *I'll talk to her at lunch. How hard could it be to tell my sister that I was sorry for treating her like shit for over twenty years?* Our discussion was a regular sisterly conversation in which I explained how regretful I was of my past behavior towards her in treating her like a leper and for not treating her with love and kindness during certain periods in my life. Jenny just smiled at me and told me she loved me, and knew that I wasn't that same person anymore, and that she was happy I was sober. My amends to her was as effortlessness as purchasing my pair of *True Religion* jeans at Nordstrom's minutes prior.

Conversely, in facing Suzy for the same purpose, I found it a smidgen more self-effacing and complex. Since I knew there were many specific incidents, I had written each one down, that I could remember with six months of sobriety. I proceeded to make apologies for not being as good a friend as I should have been, specifically sleeping with her boyfriend, Sean, while she was at college and among other occurrences where I had treated her poorly. She accepted my atonements with a smile, but then pointed out other things that I didn't even realize. She commented how the consistent lying and manipulation that I brought into our friendship seemed trivial to me, but to her it meant that I had no respect for her as a close friend. I was humbled and obliged to her. She was right. I explained to her that I didn't have to behave this way anymore since I was a different person now. Our discussion was tearful and heartfelt, which provided us with a stronger bond as friends. Suzy trusts me, listens to me, and understands me now in a healthier light.

You do the amends for yourself so you can feel relief from any guilt and gain closure for all the fucked-up shit you did to others in your past life. I made a couple face-to-face amends with ex-boyfriends, but I also sent letters to them, as well as emails and phone calls. Making amends to my dad, mom and brother was just as difficult. But in the end, I felt at peace and content about following through with this vital step, and in knowing that I did go back and try to repair my past, to the best of my ability.

In the early months of my sobriety, I was discreet as to what information I shared with my family about getting sober and in living in recovery. I spoke to Jenny almost daily, and she was fully aware of what I was going through, especially my social life in the fellowship. When I told her and my mother about my diagnosis of being bi-polar, neither one seemed too surprised. My mother was more concerned about the legal ramifications as a result of my DUI than my evolution in getting sober. My sentence included a restricted license, allowing me to drive to and from work, to twelve hours of group therapy sessions, and attend a DUI education class-- where they stressed and enforced not drinking and driving, but didn't address whether or not anyone had a drinking problem. I also appeared in court to plead guilty and had to pay a fine of $1,850.00, which I had to borrow from my mother.

My brother, Bobby, didn't really acknowledge that I was getting sober, whereas my father was encouraging me every step of the way to stay on the sobriety path and understood what efforts were involved. He kept saying how proud he was of me, and when I would joke about drinking again, he would get very adamant for me not to do so. It was comforting to know that he grasped the magnitude of what I was accomplishing. He identified with me, on some level, maybe knowing better than anyone else how difficult it was for me to get sober, since he and I shared similar traits. Suzy too was supportive and inquired frequently about the program, the twelve steps and the fellowship. I was soon to experience what it would be like in the presence of my whole family -- sober.

Chapter 20

October 2004
First visit back home — sober
Valley Forge, Pennsylvania

At almost six months sober, I had a business trip scheduled to New Jersey in early October, which happened to coincide with an engagement party for my brother, who was getting married again the following March. I extended my trip into the weekend so I could visit with my family. I was nervous to see them sober, but also excited to see them and be sober around them, which I knew would be difficult. I didn't know how to act sober around my family. I hadn't been sober around them for over twenty years. Whether or not I was actually drinking when I was with my family, I wasn't sober.

I may not have had alcohol in my system, but it was still lodged into the tissue of my brain and it hindered my thought process. I didn't have the same alcoholic thinking anymore and now it would be tested. Sharon suggested that when I was around my family to be an observer. To not comment on how they were acting or what they were doing, but to just be present and enjoy being around them, as difficult as it may be. My family is always running at high velocity, and it's hard to get your voice heard. I didn't want to be the dunce in the corner, but I also didn't want to be antagonistic. So, I just sat and listened, as long as I could. When I found myself uncomfortable or irritated, I would leave, call an AA friend or Sharon, bitch about my family and smoke a cigarette, and if need be run to a meeting. I went to meetings in Valley Forge daily and saw some people I knew from my heyday—no surprise there—but it was comforting to be amongst other alcoholics.

Bobby's engagement party was held at a long-time friend's home, and I knew I would see a lot of my brother's friends that I hadn't seen in months or even years. Some of them I had even, gulp, slept with, at one point in my life. Very humiliating remembering that, and being sober really made me realize just how careless and screwed up I had been. Suzy was my date, and was happy to be. I'd told her I needed her there with me since I was nervous about going. I drove to the party with Jenny and told her I'd be her designated driver, and she seemed relieved to know that. You have to realize that my family drinks at every function, and that my getting sober didn't change their drinking or socializing, and why should it? Alcoholism was my problem, not theirs. I didn't want anyone not to drink around me, unless they wanted to support me that way. I wasn't expecting special treatment.

Arriving at the party, I was dressed in my best high-end hip attire. My exterior fashion draped me like bougainvillea around a trestle, and I felt secure and subdued. This feeling changed within minutes of entering the home.

I walked into the kitchen, which led into a great room that was decorated in upscale Pottery Barn décor. On the kitchen counter, all I could see was bottles. Bottles of wine, bottles of vodka, bottles of champagne, bottles upon bottles of booze! Yikes, my enemy was waiting for me. It was calling out to me in a sophisticated and romantic setting. It looked harmless, but it whet my palate. I was shocked with how much liquor was there. Is this how much alcohol was normally served at gatherings I attended? No, it couldn't be.

Yes it could be. This was the standard quantity at all parties I attended. I knew this because I would survey the alcohol supply as soon as I entered a party; that was always the first thing I looked for. *How much booze is here? Is there enough for me?* When I would attend parties, before I got sober, I would hide a bottle of wine for myself, just in case they ran out. I had to make sure that I would be taken care of.

Margaret was the host and someone I had grown up with, as she and my brother were in the same crowd. She was married and had triplets. I thought my sister had it rough with twins, but Margaret was very capable and a great mother and wife to her family. She knew I was sober and was careful not to address it in front of the others. I had called her earlier in the day to see if I could bring anything, and she mentioned that Bobby had told her I got sober, and she was more than understanding. I told her I'd bring some Red Bull as my choice beverage, and not to worry about having anything for me to drink.

Hugging me, "Nance, I'm so glad to see you. You look great; you look five years younger, Wow! How is life treating you in California?"

Shy and not able to accept compliments as well as I should, I said, "Thanks Mags, it's great to see you, and yeah I feel great. Life is good, San Diego is good."

"Well good for you. Let me take those Red Bulls off your hands and put them in the fridge." Margaret opened the fridge to discover it was stocked with food and beer without an inch of space to add anything else, especially a non-alcoholic beverage.

"Hmph, I can't find any room in here to put that. Here, I'll stash it out in the garage for you."

Great, my beverage has been banished to the garage. "Ok, that's fine, no worries, and thanks." I felt like an outsider. The party ensued for the next half-hour greeting long-lost friends, and in spite of this I felt awkward without an alcohol beverage in my hand. I didn't have my liquid courage to give me the poise and confidence I so desperately needed. I hadn't been around alcohol in a social setting since I got sober, and this was a new environment for me to be in. I felt like I was fifteen years old at the High School mixer, and no one was asking me to dance.

My brother had a friend who was sober, not through AA, but on his own accord. He'd been having black-outs frequently and knew he needed to quit, so he quit on his own and found Catholicism again; whatever it takes. He brought non-alcoholic red wine to the party and knew I quit drinking also. He poured some for himself and asked if I wanted to have a glass. I figured sure, why not, it can't hurt, and I'll feel more comfortable at the party with a wine glass in my hand. I was nervous taking a sip, and it tasted like cheap red wine. I remembered that taste and I liked it, which made me leery about drinking it. I remembered hearing about how people would relapse on non-alcoholic beer and wine and thinking that could happen to me. I was concerned that I would pick up somebody else's wine glass that looked like mine, and then it'd be all over. I thought about just drinking then and saying screw it, I'll get sober again when I get back to San Diego, this is just too difficult. If I can drink this glass of non-alcoholic wine, why not just drink a normal glass? One glass won't hurt.

I looked at Suzy and she asked, "How is it? Is it weird? Are you sure you should be drinking that?"

I stood and thought and put it down and looked at her. "You know, I can't drink this, it's too slippery of a slope for me. It'll make me want to drink a real glass of wine."

Suzy nodded knowingly, grabbed my arm and said, "Okay let's go downstairs and have a cigarette, we need to get you outta the kitchen." I was grateful for her response in understanding the importance of that defining moment for me. Right there I truly surrendered and knew that God put a test in front of me—I passed.

When I came home over the Christmas holiday, again, the season was full of family gatherings and parties, and with a couple more months of sobriety under my belt, it wasn't as difficult. It was trying at times, but I wanted to be sober more than I wanted to drink.

Back in San Diego, I was entering 2005 with a whole new outlook on my life, one that I was eagerly awaiting. I spent New Year's Eve with Ben and some other friends playing Scrabble until 2:30 A.M. If someone had told me the prior New Year's that I'd be sober and playing a board game, I would have thought they were smoking crack.

April 1, 2005
Kella's Relapse
Carlsbad, California

In February, both Kella and Diana took
One Year tokens, and it was magical. I cried
when I presented each of them with their
tokens, and I was very proud of them and
delighted that they were both in my life. Kella
had a rough first year in sobriety. In divorcing
her husband of ten years and selling their
dream home, she was now faced with having
to change her life completely as a single
mother and finding a job in the marketplace, in
addition to being sober. Kella started dating
someone soon after she left her husband, and
on the outside seemed happy, but I knew
something wasn't right with her. She kept it all
inside and wasn't sharing fully what was going
on in her head. She wasn't honest with me or
her sponsor either.

One Saturday morning, after she and I
attended a meeting at Second Street, we had
planned to go to a meeting in downtown San
Diego; however, she changed her mind at the
last minute and told me she wasn't going to go.
I was pissed and said *fine, do what you want* and
then went on my merry way—alone, I might

add. After I came home from the afternoon meeting in San Diego, I called her. No answer. I didn't hear back from her for a few hours and then called her again that night; again, I didn't hear back from her. This behavior from her was unusual because we never failed to return each other's calls.

The next morning was Easter Sunday and Kella was celebrating it with her family in the traditional holiday manner. She called me and asked if I wanted to spend the Holiday with her and her family, and when she spoke to me, she wasn't her normal self. She was acting odd. I already had Easter plans with Sharon, so I declined, but when I asked her what she did the prior night, she was evasive. I blew it off and went on about my day, wondering what really happened, but I knew she'd tell me at her own pace.

My worst fear was that she was *thinking* of taking some Adderall that she commented to me was in her household, or that she had cheated on her boyfriend with someone from the program. Kella was a flirt who could charm anyone, and she was getting bored with her current suitor. I wasn't prepared for what occurred next. A couple of hours later Kella called me, crying and upset.

"Hi......did you hear?" She asked.

"Hear what? What are you talking about?" I heard a shoe drop and instinctively knew she had been drinking. I started shaking, "Honey, what happened?"

Crying she replied, "I went out...." This means you've relapsed. "...and I drank. I'm drinking."

Two weeks after Kella took her One Year token, she started popping pills. Her son was taking Atterall, a drug used to treat hyperactivity in children, and two weeks earlier she had swiped some of his pills, like any good mother would. Taking the Atterall had propelled her craving to want to start drinking.

In responding to her over the phone on her admission that she drank, I tried to remain calm and let her feel that this was normal. "Okay, it's okay. I'm going to the 6:00 P.M. meeting; do you want to come with me?"

My mind was scurrying, and all I could think of was taking her to a meeting. What do I do? Should I go over to her house? Should I call Sharon? What? I wasn't equipped to deal with this. Her children had left her house hours earlier and were now with her ex-husband, Justin.

"No I don't want to go to the meeting, I'm not stopping. Will you call Justin for me and tell him not to bring the kids home?"

Shocked, I thought, she's not going to stop drinking? She wants me to call Justin to tell him that she's drinking and for him to keep the kids? Was she serious? Of course she was. Once an alcoholic starts drinking, the craving is awakened and it's difficult to stop. Very difficult.

"Sure, I'll call him, what's his number?" Seconds later, I asked, "Kella, do you want me to come over?"

I was now shaking and starting to cry, fearful of what I would find if I walked into her home. I knew Kella did drugs in addition to drinking, and it wouldn't be a safe environment to insert myself into.

Kella still had her wits though. "I don't think that's a good idea. I'm using and this isn't a good place for you to be. You should call your sponsor. I don't want you to jeopardize your sobriety."

Okay, good she's thinking. But something about going to her house and seeing beer and coke or meth, whatever she was snorting, sounded appealing to me. Holding back tears, I started pacing and thinking. I wasn't sure what I wanted to do—did I want to be in that environment? No, I wanted my friend sober again.

Going full throttle, I said, "Ok, I'm going to call Sharon and see what she says. I don't like the idea of you home alone and me not being able to help you. Let me see what she says."

Kella replied, "Oh, I'm not alone, Lucas is on his way back."

Lucas was a member of the fellowship who had relapsed a couple of days earlier. It all made sense to me now. She had planned to relapse with him, and subconsciously or not, this is what happened. Nothing happens by coincidence.

"Oh nice. Jesus. I'll call you back in a minute, and I'll call Justin for you."
I was annoyed, but also scared for her. Lucas wasn't a high-bottom drunk; he was a hard core drug user and alcoholic. She was putting herself in harm's way and didn't care about what could happen. That is how most alcoholics relapse; they plan it out, whether or not they realize it. In hearing people share why and how they relapsed, they mainly explain that they'd stop going to meetings, stop calling their sponsor, weren't being honest

with themselves or were holding onto a secret or a resentment toward someone, but most likely, they stopped praying and had lost contact with the man upstairs. In Kella's case, she wasn't being honest with who she was and what was going on in her head. She lost her will to pray, and she got the fuck-its. Fuck-it, who cares? I wanna drink and no one's going to stop me.

Throughout the ordeal, alcohol was calling to me, not because I wanted to drink, so much as that I felt I *needed* to drink. My fidgety body and racing mind were telling me that in order to handle such a crisis, I had to have a drink. I almost went over to Kella's house. Instead, I called Sharon to get her perspective, thinking she would be understanding and gentle.

No, she was adamant, "No way are you going over there. If you were to go over there, you'd need to bring a couple of other women with you. But no way are you going over there alone. Call her back and tell her you will call Justin for her. And then tell her to call you when she's sober. You can't be part of her relapse. It's not healthy for you and your sobriety. You can't associate yourself with her.

Call me back. I want to make sure you're not getting involved with this. "

I was a little shocked at her response and really didn't understand it. Aren't I supposed to be a friend to her, no matter what? I was not going to turn my back on her. I wanted to drive over to her house so bad and see how she was and really see what was going on; I was a little intrigued. Exciting drunken drama. Sounded like old times. I called Justin and he didn't seem too surprised. He said she was acting peculiar earlier in the day and that he knew something was going on. He agreed to keep the kids until she got her head out of her ass. I called her back and told her what Sharon and Justin had said. She seemed okay with it. I pleaded with her to stop drinking and to come to the evening meeting with me. By then she was fully into her drinking and drugging spree. She hadn't slept in over twenty-four hours and had no desire to stop.

The last thing I said to her on the phone was, "Okay, I love you and call me when you can. But please do not drink and drive. DUIs suck."

Six hours later, Justin called me.

"Hi Nancy, its Justin. Have you talked to Kella?" He sounded defeated.

By then it was close to 11:00 P.M. and I was getting ready for bed. I answered the phone hesitantly. "Hi Justin....No, I haven't heard from her, why? What's going on?"

Frustrated, Justin said, "Kella's in jail; she got a DUI."

"Oh fuck, are you kidding me? God damn it, I told her not to drive, I can't freaking believe this. Well, do you know what happened?"

"Not really, she got it about a mile from the house. I have to pick her up in the morning, or whenever they let her out. The car had to be towed away; that's all I know."

"Okay, well call me if you need to and let me know what I can do to help out. I can't believe this. She's relapsed for what, thirty-six hours and gets her ass in jail already? I hung up the phone and felt sad for her, but more irritated than sad. What the fuck was she thinking? *Oh that's right, we're not thinking when we're wasted; we think we're invincible.* I remembered that feeling.

The next morning Kella called me when she got out of jail and told me what occurred. She had run out of beer and was driving to the local pharmacy to get more. Drunk, she was swerving on the road and hit a cable box. Her car stopped and steam started rising from her engine. She sat and thought what to do. She cut out a line on her center console, took a swig from her beer and called Triple A to see if they could come and tow her. Minutes later a tow truck driver from Triple A showed up and surveyed the scene. He quickly realized that he had a drunk driver on his hands and phoned the police. Seconds later a cop showed up and asked if she'd been drinking. Here was the funny part: Kella replied she'd only had a couple of beers and that she was a member of Alcoholics Anonymous and could control her liquor.

The cop shined the flashlight into her car and found at least eight empty crushed beer cans on the floor. Kella was taken into custody and hauled to jail. What Kella neglected to tell the cop was that she also had a baggie of meth in her jeans pocket and they didn't strip search her.

Kella was sad, but also laughing a little about the story to me. I knew she was going straight to the pharmacy to get more beer, and as sure as a pig is pink, she did. She continued calling me that day and was crying, mostly when she called, and just saying she loved me and couldn't stop. By now she had barricaded herself into her home and was drinking and using. She had been up for almost three days and as much as her family, her sponsor, her ex-husband and I tried to get her stop; she couldn't. This cycle went on for a couple more days, and then finally, on the seventh day, she stopped.

During Kella's relapse, a number of people told me that she might not come back to the Program. Not everyone who relapses comes back. Some would keep drinking for years after getting sober their first time, and sometimes they'd come back to AA only much later to get sober again, or worse yet they can die. They also told me not to be an enabler to her and engage in any communication with her, as this would not be helpful to her or me. If I cut her out of my life, she'd be in more pain and more alone and hopefully surrender to herself and admit that she needed help again. She called me a lot during her relapse, and as difficult as it was, I wouldn't answer my phone. The one time I did answer my phone, we both just cried, and I told her not to call me until she was sober again.

A week later she got sober again and I picked her up at her house to take her to a meeting. When I got out of my car and walked towards her, I saw a different person, wounded and humbled, a piece of my friend was missing. In the coming weeks Kella slipped a couple of times and drank for an hour or two, but she always came back. Kella had a lot of wreckage to repair from her devastating relapse, but she came back a changed woman.

As I eliminated alcohol from my life, both as a crutch and as a "necessity," I realized with growing clarity how difficult the challenges to sobriety could be. Triggers were tricky since certain people and places would pop into my head and make me remember *what it was like*. I had a lot of triggers and still do. Driving through Del Mar, I would see the locales of specific bars and restaurants and recall vivid memories of my prior life of drinking and drugging. The actual evening would unfold in my mind to the extent that I would sometimes find myself longing for what I used to have. Twenty minutes of relief. Those first few minutes of drinking brought me initial pleasure. Having a glass of wine in a nice restaurant enabled me to feel like a normal participant in a socially acceptable environment. However, I would mentally fast forward to 2:00 A.M. where the lunacy found me looking for solace with anyone handy at the local dive bar. Thankfully when these fantasies would occur, I could retreat into my sober thinking and be thankful that I didn't have to live like that anymore.

Triggers happen a lot, and in the beginning of my sobriety almost everything was a trigger – first sober visit with the family, first sober Christmas first sober New Years Eve, first sober wedding, first sober birthday and the first time visit with old friend.

Kimberly, my greatly admired old childhood friend, the one who introduced me to marijuana and cocaine, was coming to town for a visit.

Chapter 21

May 11, 2005 – One Year Sober
San Diego Airport
San Diego, California

Kimberly, still a dear friend, supported me in my efforts to get sober, and had decided to fly down from the Bay Area for my one year AA birthday! What a change from our teenage years of drug and alcohol experimentation. It only took me twenty-four years to finally walk away from that experiment. Kimberly tempered her conduct after college and barely drank a glass of wine with dinner. She and I spoke every few weeks throughout our friendship, which had endured the test of time and distance, but when I talked to her, I would often lie about how I was living my life. Rationalizing all my behaviors to her, I only shared a glimpse of my reality with her. Kimberly knew me well, however, and could hear in my voice that my life wasn't a page out of *Good Housekeeping*. When I was arrested for my second DUI, I decided to tell Kimberly. She was concerned for me and wanted me to get help. I mentioned that I might go to AA, and she encouraged me in my decision and started calling me every day to see how I was doing.

Kimmy was proud of me on my one year milestone, so much so, that she took a day out of her life to fly down and spend my special day with me. It was touching to have such a great friend in my life.

As I drove to the airport to pick up Kimmy, I aptly remembered it was exactly one year ago *that day* when I had flown into San Diego from Philadelphia sober–and willing to try sobriety. I knew that I was not that same person driving to the airport. A smile curved across my face as I pulled up to the terminal to get Kimmy. She arrived curbside from her flight and hopped into my car. She commented that I looked healthier and emanated a glow of confidence and purpose. We hugged and sped off towards Encinitas, chatting away like we hadn't missed a day.

I lit a cigarette and opened the sunroof of my new vehicle, a used Lexus coupe that my Dad shipped to me for my One Year. What a great gift to get from him – he was so proud of me and wanted to do anything he could for me. I finally got rid of my Honda, with all the bad memories that car held; it was great to discard a piece of my past life.

"Okay, this is the agenda for the day. We are going to a noon meeting at Second Street, where I will receive a token for my year. Then you, Kella and I are going to Poseidon for a beachside lunch, and then we'll run around Del Mar and do some shopping? Sound like a plan?"

Kimmy seemed comfortable that I had planned the day and all she had to do was show up. "Nance, that sounds great. I'm glad I'll get to meet Kella. But explain to me the taking of the token again; I don't get it."

"Yeah, it's different everywhere, but in San Diego it's all about you – it's a bit much, but hey this is So Cal. For me being the center of attention is kind of nerve-wracking, but when you have a milestone 'birthday' in AA for each year of sobriety a person presents you with a token and a cake. The way someone would for a birthday. The symbolism is kind of elementary, but it's significant to us."

She nodded, "Okay, I understand it. But what does the person do that is presenting you with the cake and token?"

"Right, they say their name first, 'Hi, I'm Kella; I'm an alcoholic;' everyone chants back, 'Hi, Kella.' Ya know that whole introduction thing. Then Kella, or the

311

presenter, talks about the person they are giving the token to. 'This is Nancy. I met Nancy when she had two weeks of sobriety and blah, blah, blah.' Kella gives me the token and then I speak. I talk about what the last year has meant to me, how it was to get sober and really whatever I want to say."

Kimmy seemed enthused, "OK, this will be cool. I will get to see Kella give you your one-year token."

As soon as Kimmy said that, I was panic-stricken, knowing that I would have to speak in front of others. I needed another cigarette. Kimmy and I got out of the car as I parked across the street from the Second Street Fellowship. I looked over to her and she smiled. She walked over to me, grabbed me and hugged me.

"Nance, I am so very proud of you and you should be proud of you too. I am so glad you have finally put your life back together."

I looked at her and tears flooded my eyes. "I'm glad that you're here to see this and I love you. I also want you to know that I have never felt you were the catalyst for my partying life. You are my oldest and dearest friend, the one who saw me smoke my first joint, snort my first line and let me lie to you

for years about my drugging and drinking –
and you loved me in spite of all that. The fact
that you went through your party phase and
stopped after college made me want to emulate
you. But, I just couldn't get to that point, until
now."

Kimmy, slightly tilting her head to the
side while clasping my hands, said, "Nance, I
never judged you, so please don't think I did
just because I was able to walk away from that
lifestyle. Life is life and things happen.
C'mon, let's go in and see you take your
token."

We started walking towards "the
clubhouse," as fellowship members facetiously
called the dingy, wood-paneled room with
resin chairs that seated fifty-five at full
capacity. The room had a small driveway in
front to separate the smokers who stood by the
entrance before the meeting would commence.
This unattractive room was the last house on
the block for me, my safe house. I had such a
strong connection to this magical place.
Kimmy and I took a seat close to the front
where the secretary and leader sat; they both
directed the meeting. Minutes later, Kella
walked in, beaming, and I introduced Kimmy
to her. Kella sat behind me.

"Are you nervous? I can't believe it's been a year. I'm so excited for you."

I smiled to her. "Yeah a full year, I'm just as shocked as anybody. Freaking me out, actually."

A part of me felt guilty that I had achieved my year, knowing that I hadn't relapsed. Kella barely had thirty days of sobriety under her belt with her relapse from last month. But, I knew my path was different than hers, and so was my story. The fact that I didn't relapse in my first year astounded me. I kept saying to myself every day, *Amazing, I didn't have to drink today ….and it's a Saturday*! I'd come very close to relapsing when Kella did, and luckily my sponsor told me to stay close to the other women in the program who had more sober time than I had and listen to what they had to say. My ass was falling off and they carried me for a few weeks. My guilt of having a full year of sobriety, where Kella had failed, left when the meeting started, yet the butterflies were surely fluttering around in my stomach.

Kella stood in front of the room. "This is Nancy. I met Nancy a couple weeks into her sobriety, and we have talked every day on the phone ever since. She is my best friend and my rock. I am so blessed to have her in my life and to be my teacher. I love you with all my heart. Congratulations!" Kella gave me my One Year two-sided token that read, "To Thine Own Self be True," with the terms Service, Unity and Recovery circling the AA triangle logo. The other side had the Serenity prayer engraved. Kella hugged me, and Kimmy wiped a tear. Hugging Kella back, I started tearing up myself. It had been such a tough year and an emotional one as well. Thank goodness there was a box of tissues behind me on the desk. There are always a lot of tears at AA meetings.

Kella took her seat. I turned to her. "Thank you Kella for this token; you helped me more than you know this year. I love you and you mean a lot to me. Wow, I can't believe this." Looking at the token, I was in awe and trembled as I spoke. "I didn't come to my first meeting to get sober. I came to get a piece of paper signed to appease the courts for my second DUI. But what I found here has exceeded what I ever thought was possible for me. I found a new way to live my life—and be sober and be a woman with dignity, integrity and honesty. I came into this room and surrendered my will and dove into this program. I got a sponsor, I worked the steps, and I became a different person. And I started to like myself a whole lot more than when I walked through that door a year ago today. I'm truly grateful to be here and grateful to be an alcoholic. Thank you."

I sat down and my heart was racing and I thought this is truly a gift. I looked outside the window and up into the sky and said *Thank You* to whatever was out there. I knew I hadn't done this all on my own.

Chapter 22

May 11, 2009
Five years sober
Encinitas, California

Since May 2004 a lot in my life has changed; it's been an inside job. I know to my core that I am an alcoholic, and nothing will change that. In looking back at my alcohol career, I feel I probably crossed over in my late teens. They say there is a time for most alcoholics where you cross over into the powerless part, and you can't control your drinking or behavior. Some people believe that you are born with an alcoholic gene and some others feel you push and you push and then you're at the point of no return. When I was out there drinking and using, I felt like a thirsty sponge that would get squeezed out sporadically only to fill up again to keep forging ahead. After I went through my crazy twenties, I began to figure out how to incorporate my drug and alcohol use to accommodate my career and life. This was when I felt it gave me the illusion of being more manageable. And if you, my mom, my dad, my sister, or my boyfriend had approached me on my abuse of alcohol and cocaine, I would have told you to fuck off. Up until May 11, 2004, no one could have told me I needed help.

Alcohol was what I used to make me feel better, or to not feel at all. It's amazing to me that the elimination of my most cherished medicine is what would make my life worth living. Who knew that taking alcohol out of my system would let me see the light? I can't imagine what my life would be today if I had not stopped drinking when I did. I had to make the conscious decision that I wanted to stop. I had no idea what I was in for and figured I'd dry out for a couple of weeks.

That God works in mysterious ways is an understatement. I know, with as much certainty that I'm an alcoholic, that if I never got my second DUI, I would still be living in my disease. My second DUI was a blessing in disguise—divine intervention is what I believe. Because as much as I was trying to sustain my life of continued drinking and drugging, I needed to have another consequence jar my brain to finally wake me up. I kept rationalizing the way I was living my life and not thinking anything was wrong with it, when deep down I knew it wasn't healthy.

The day I surrendered and turned my life over is the day I said enough. I came into the program willing to do whatever I could to have a better life. Someone told me at one of my first meetings, "You'll never have to feel that way again." Those were the magic words for me. I would never have to feel less than or not good enough or that something was wrong with me. I know now what is wrong with me and what a relief it is. I'm a grateful recovering alcoholic. I finally found what I was searching for my whole life. Me.

My sobriety birthday is the most precious date in my life. More important to me than my belly-button birthday or Christmas. It marks the date I found a new way to live life with purpose.

Living life in recovery each day is an awakening and the beginning of where you get to practice the steps and spiritual principles in your career, relationships, and life. It's no wonder they say in the program, *Don't leave before the miracle happens*. Because anyone that can quit drinking and doing drugs, at least the way I did, is a miracle in itself. I'm finally at a place where I feel good about the choices I make in my life, and I am happy with the person I've become.

Today I'm someone that gets invited to parties because they want me to attend! Quite the switch from my life before I got sober. Today I am going to attend a 5 year Anniversary-Birthday AA party for me. I'm lucky that I have amazing friends that love and value me. I'm truly blessed that my family sent their well wishes and a gift earlier this week and they too seem grateful that I'm sober -- and accounted for.

For the first time in my life, I actually like who I see in the mirror. I am truly living a life of freedom, integrity and love. I have a sense of self and can hold my head up high when I walk into a restaurant and not wonder who saw me out the night before and what I did and with whom. I can live my life like this, if I want to—one day at a time. Because that's all I've got.

Epilogue

In November 2003, I was drunk, typing in my journal and at that time, I hadn't admitted to myself yet that I was an alcoholic. I thought I was just a problem drinker – which is also another term for an alcoholic. I wanted to write about my frustration of not being married and blame it on someone. In getting prepared to embark on another move across the country, I wanted to find something that would repair the gaping hole I felt inside. I thought that if I had the perfect life of husband, house, dog and child -- life would work out and I would be part of the suburbia landscape with the general population. It wasn't until I got sober that I decided to take control of my life and —be responsible for my actions. This may in turn answer my non-married question, but it may not. I wasn't involved with healthy people, so why should my relationships have been healthy with the promise of any future?

When I originally wrote my story, I was in early sobriety and I'm now over 13 years sober and life is in session. Today I like to say I have Cadillac problems. I don't need to be bailed out of a Jail for any DUIs, I know where

I am when I wake up in the morning, and I have a little more self respect and dignity than I used to. Progress. Just because I'm sober doesn't mean life doesn't get *lifey*. Good things happen. Bad things happen. They just normally don't happen on the same day. And no matter what, I've been able to stay sober through all of it. It's not easy, but as long as I keep doing what I was taught to do by others that walked before me, I know I'm going to be ok.

My ex-boyfriend, Matty got sober a couple years after I did and he's currently married to an amazing girl and we get to be sober friends and that's pretty darn cool. I'm still friends with all the women I got sober with, in addition to Kimmy and Suzy and they are my biggest supporters. It's all good.

Good things have happened. I rescued a Boxer mix (Lucy – named after a GD song) in 2008; she was the second best decision I ever made. She lets me love her unconditionally and she's basically my child (yes I've turned into one of those dog people). I landed a great job in my industry and they value me as much as I value them. I have been able to re-establish my relationships with family and friends and in the process have made amazing sober new friends that truly get me.

And of course, some bad things happened. In 2010, I left my safety zone of sunny San Diego and moved back East when my Mother was diagnosed with FTD (front temporal lobe) Dementia. I was able to spend time with her and be a loving, helpful and sober daughter to her. Sadly, Mom passed away two years later, but I was so grateful that I was able to be there for her and my family. It was difficult going through her death, but I was sober through all of it and truly blessed I didn't feel a need to drink through it.

Then more good things happened; I met someone at an AA meeting. We got married 18 months later – he was the third best decision I ever made.

In 2004, I was tired and had run out of excuses. I gave sobriety a chance. It was complete blind faith and it surely paid off.

That was the best decision I ever made.

APPENDIX

AA Preamble

Alcoholics Anonymous is a fellowship of men and women who share their experience, strength and hope with each other that they may solve their common problem and help others to recover from alcoholism.

The only requirement for membership is a desire to stop drinking. There are no dues or fees for A.A. membership; we are self supporting through our own contributions. A.A. is not allied with any sect, denomination, politics, organization or institution; does not wish to engage in any controversary, neither endorses nor opposes any causes. Our primary purpose is to stay sober and help other alcoholics to achieve sobriety.**

Where to get help

Most AA meetings are open to the public, as well as to recovering alcoholics. Some meetings are only open to alcoholics, or to people that have a desire to stop drinking. The best way to find a meeting is to go online at www.aa.org and you can find a meeting in any town, state or country.

There are numerous treatment and rehabilitation centers throughout the country, and most insurance plans offer coverage for substance abuse/mental health.

You can also contact:
AA World Service Headquarters:
P.O. Box 459
Grand Central Station
New York, NY 10163
(212) 870-3400

Additionally, there are movies and books* that you can read that may assist you in determining if you think you could have a problem:

Books:

> Drinking, a Love Story, Caroline Knapp
> Dry, Augusten Burroughs
> A Drinking Life, Pete Hammill
> Alcoholics Anonymous (the Big Book)

Movies:

> When a Man Loves a Woman
> 28 Days
> Clean and Sober
> Flight
> Leaving Las Vegas
> My Name is Bill W.

These movies and books are my suggestions only.

**AA is what worked to get me sober. I don't endorse it as the only means to get sober; it's just what worked for me. There are other options available out there.*

Get in Touch with me:

Feel free to contact me on my Facebook page, Nancy Carr or the page for "Last Call"

Email me directly at nlcarr@outlook.com

Feel free to review my blog at http://lastcallblog.me

Made in the USA
Middletown, DE
20 May 2018